BRIGHT NOTES

ONE HUNDRED YEARS OF SOLITUDE BY GABRIEL GARCÍA MÁRQUEZ

Intelligent Education

Nashville, Tennessee

BRIGHT NOTES: One Hundred Years Of Solitude
www.BrightNotes.com

No part of this publication may be used or reproduced in any manner whatsoever without written permission, except in the case of brief quotations in critical articles and reviews. For permissions, contact Influence Publishers http://www.influencepublishers.com.

ISBN: 978-1-645421-44-3 (Paperback)
ISBN: 978-1-645421-45-0 (eBook)

Published in accordance with the U.S. Copyright Office Orphan Works and Mass Digitization report of the register of copyrights, June 2015.

Originally published by Monarch Press.
Geoffrey E. Fox, 1967
2019 Edition published by Influence Publishers.

Interior design by Lapiz Digital Services. Cover Design by Thinkpen Designs.

Printed in the United States of America.

Library of Congress Cataloging-in-Publication Data forthcoming.
Names: Intelligent Education
Title: BRIGHT NOTES: One Hundred Years Of Solitude
Subject: STU004000 STUDY AIDS / Book Notes

CONTENTS

1)	Gabriel García Márquez: The Man and His Times	1
2)	Introduction to Gabriel García Márquez	23
3)	Introduction to One Hundred Years of Solitude	36
4)	Textual Analysis	
	Chapters 1–3	61
	Chapters 4–12	73
	Chapters 13–20	91
5)	Character Analyses	109
6)	Critical and Political Reputation	125
7)	Essay Questions and Answers	136
8)	Bibliography	145

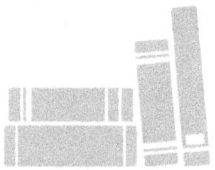

INTRODUCTION TO GABRIEL GARCÍA MÁRQUEZ

"MY NAME, SIR..."

In 1966, while he was writing *One Hundred Years of Solitude*, the author introduced himself to readers of a short story anthology with these words:

> **My name, sir, is Gabriel García Márquez.... I was born in Aracataca, Colombia, almost forty years ago and I still do not regret it. My sign is Pisces and my woman Mercedes. Those are the two most important things that have occurred in my life, because thanks to those, at least up to now, I have managed to survive by writing.**

He claimed he was "a writer because of shyness" and that, if he hadn't been so clumsy, he would have followed his "true vocation" as prestidigitator. In either case, only one thing interested him: "to make my friends love me more."

Writing did not come easily, he assured the reader. "I have had to subject myself to an atrocious discipline to finish half a page in eight hours of work; I fight every word with punches and the word almost always wins," although he was "so stubborn" he had "managed to publish four books in twenty years." Then he concluded on an angrier, eerie note:

> I never talk about literature, because I don't know what it is and, besides, I am convinced that the world would be the same without it. On the other hand, I am convinced the world would be completely different if the police didn't exist. I think, then, that I would have been more useful to humanity if instead of a writer I were a terrorist.

[*Los diez mandamientos*. Buenos Aires: Editorial Jorge Alvarez, 1966; quoted in Fernandez-Brasso, 1982:28–29.]

A CHILDHOOD AMONG GHOSTS AND LEGENDS

Aracataca is a small town a few miles south of Cienaga, in the hot northern coastal area of Colombia and not far, incidentally, from a town named Soledad ("Solitude"). There, Gabriel Jose García Márquez was born on either March 6, 1928 - as he has said - or March 6, 1927 - as his father told Harley D. Oberhelman in a 1977 interview; the author himself told reporters he "wasn't sure" of his birthdate (v. Oberhelman 1980:18).

His father, Gabriel Eligio García, had come to the town to work as a telegrapher during the "banana fever," when the United Fruit Company's commercial exploitation of bananas created many kinds of jobs and brought a brief era of prosperity to the zone. His mother was Luisa Santiaga Márquez Iguaran, daughter of Colonel Nicolas Márquez Iguaran and of Tranquilina Iguaran Cotes, the colonel's wife and first cousin.

The colonel objected strongly to his daughter's poor and illegitimate suitor (who was also reputed to be a ladies' man) and had tried to prevent the marriage, using his considerable influence to have the telegrapher transferred to Riohacha, a rather distant town. Nevertheless, the couple carried on their romance over the telegraph wires and in secret meetings, and when her parents finally consented to their marriage, Luisa Santiaga went to live with her husband in Riohacha. She returned to her parents' home just long enough to bear the child, whom she left with her parents when she and her husband went back to Riohacha.

First Of Twelve Children

Thus it was that Gabriel García Márquez, or "Gabito" or "Gabo" as he was known, spent the first years of his life in the big house of his grandparents. Gabriel Eligio García and Luisa Santiaga Márquez would have six more sons and five daughters, but their firstborn would hardly know them until he was much older. In fact, his first memory of his mother is from when he was five or six (Vargas Llosa, 1971:21).

He would live in Aracataca until the death of his grandfather in 1936, when Gabo was eight or nine. He has said on many occasions that his grandfather was the most important figure in his life, and that after the colonel's death and his own departure from the big house in Aracataca, "nothing interesting has happened to me." [E. García M., 1982:98] Even if this is an exaggeration, it is true that almost all the images and personalities that dominate his early work can be traced to those early years.

Nicolas Márquez had become a colonel in the War of a Thousand Days (1899-1902), a civil war in which he fought under the command of the Liberal party General Rafael Uribe Uribe against the Conservatives (called "godos" or "Goths" by the Liberals). Many years later, Gabriel would combine his memories of his grandfather and stories he had heard about General Uribe Uribe to create the fictional character, Colonel Aureliano Buendia, who in *One Hundred Years of Solitude* launches thirty-two wars and loses them all - much as the Liberals actually had. Characters more or less modeled on the grandfather also appear in earlier stories, most noticeably *No One Writes to the Colonel*.

Model For Ursula

The (real-life) colonel had married his first cousin, Tranquilina Iguaran Cotes, some of whose traits would reappear in the fictional Ursula Iguaran, matriarch of the Buendias, and other female characters in *One Hundred Years of Solitude*. Like Ursula, grandmother Tranquilina Iguaran was a very vigorous woman who died blind and senile at a great age. Like Ursula and Fernanda del Carpio (another character in the novel), she was given to talking with people who weren't there. Intermarriage of these cousins would also be reflected in the **theme** of incest that runs through the novel.

In 1929, when Gabriel was one (or two), a great strike of banana workers in the zone around Aracataca was ended by a massacre in the train station of nearby Cienaga. The United Fruit Company had built its own irrigation system, railroad, telegraph network, retail stores, and private village for management, and had its own fleet to transport the bananas it grew in the region. However, it was evading Colombian labor law requiring medical care, sanitary housing, accident insurance, and so on, by claiming that the workers were independent producers and therefore the company had no employees. Also, in order to unload merchandise that the banana boats brought in on their return trip, the company paid workers in scrip that could be redeemed only at the company stores.

Model For The Strike In One Hundred Years Of Solitude

The strike was bitter. When the government sent in troops to do the work, the strikers resorted to sabotage (Vargas Llosa, 1971:15–21). Finally, the commanding officer, General Carlos Cortes Vargas, summoned the workers to a parlay and, when they had gathered at the railroad station in the nearby town of Cienaga, ordered them shot down. According to the general's memoirs, nine strikers were killed; according to a contemporary labor leader, 410. The "cleanup" operation by the army over the next few days killed 1,000 to 1,500 strikers or sympathizers and wounded 2,000 to 3,000 (Janes, 1981:12). The massacre ended the strike. It also ended banana production in Aracataca, whose prosperity vanished as suddenly as it had arrived.

Although Gabriel could hardly have understood these events at the time, the stories he heard about them as he was growing up made a lasting impression. His first novel, *La hojarasca (Leafstorm)*, is an impressionistic portrayal of a company's sinister impact on just such a little town. The strike and massacre would be reported much more precisely and realistically in *One Hundred Years of Solitude*. The dialogue between strikers and the army in those last minutes before the machine guns open fire on the crowd at the railroad station is taken verbatim from the memoirs of General Carlos Cortes Vargas, whose real name is used in the novel. The novel inflates the numbers of casualties, but not the horror.

Other boyhood memories that will appear in the novel include being taken by his grandfather to the circus and to a brewery (so he could discover the feel of ice), and his grandfather's relating how as a youth he had killed a man in a quarrel and how much a dead man "weighs" (on the spirit).

Personal Myths In The Novel

His grandmother Tranquilina, meanwhile, would warn the boy against disturbing the ghosts of an Aunt Petra (in the novel, Petra Cotes is a kind of fertility goddess) and an Uncle Lazaro (the fictional Melquiades, like Lazarus, will rise from the dead). Tranquilina Iguaran was also given to making up fantastic answers to the grandson's questions. Thus, when he asked who "Mambru" was, from the popular Spanish children's song "Mambru se fue a la guerra" ("Mambru went to war") she said it was someone who had fought alongside his grandfather. The truth, he found out much later, is that the song commemorates a Duke of Marlborough who fought in Spain in the early eighteenth century; mixing personal and historical myths, the novelist would give his fictitious Colonel Aureliano Buendia a bizarre comrade-in-arms named the Duke of Marlborough.

There was also an aunt who knitted her own shroud and, when she had completed it, died. This same aunt told a little girl who had found an oddly shaped chicken egg that it was a "basilisk's egg," and with great ceremony burned it in the patio (Vargas Llosa, 1971:23).

Model For Remedios The Beautiful

One of the stories the boy heard was of a family in Aracataca who, to cover up the disappearance of their attractive daughter (who probably had run away with her boyfriend), claimed that she had gone out to hang up some sheets and had mysteriously floated up to heaven. Maybe they only told that story to little boys. Anyway, Gabito was impressed, as you will see when you read about Remedios the beautiful in *One Hundred Years of Solitude*.

In 1936, Gabriel's parents moved to Sucre and sent him to a Jesuit school in Barranquilla. He then won a scholarship to study in the National Liceo (a secondary school) in Zipaquira, near Bogota in the Andes.

He found the highlanders suffocatingly pious and gloomy, in contrast to the extravagant and informal costenos (people of the coast), but endured until finishing high school in 1946. He disliked Bogota (which he has called "the ugliest city in the world") so intensely that he kept indoors as much as possible, never even visiting such famous attractions as the Cathedral of Salt. The boy was becoming well acquainted with solitude, his thoughts always on Aracataca while he refused to assimilate to this gray, chilly place where he was studying (Vargas Llosa, 1971:29-31).

BECOMING A WRITER

In 1947 he began studying law at the Universidad Nacional in Bogota ("bored to death," he has said) and published his first story, "La tercera resignacion," in the literary supplement of the newspaper *El Espectador*.

In April 1948, the popular leader of the Liberal Party, Jorge Eliecer Gaitan, was gunned down on a Bogota street and the city was convulsed by riots. Soon, open warfare between Conservative and Liberal Party supporters broke out again nationwide, as it had in the days of Gabriel's grandfather. This social and political warfare, called simply "La Violencia," much as the Irish talk of "The Troubles," would cause more than 300,000 deaths between 1949 and 1962, according to widely accepted estimates. The Universidad Nacional was closed and García Márquez moved to Cartagena, where his family had moved (his father having become a pharmacist) and where he enrolled in the university to continue his law studies. He got his first job as a reporter for a Cartagena daily, *El Universal*, and for two and a half years was reporting, studying and sending short stories to *El Espectador*.

Goodbye To Law

In 1950 he gave up his law studies definitively, moving to Barranquilla where he joined the staff of another newspaper, *El Heraldo*, writing a regular column. He fell in with a group of young writers, Alfonso Fuenmayor, Alvaro Cepeda Samudio, and German Vargas, and their mentor, the elderly Catalan professor and former book dealer Ramon Vinyes, who were a great stimulus to his reading and writing; he also met his future wife, Mercedes Barcha. (Mercedes, the three young men, and Gabriel himself, with their own names, will appear in the later pages of *One Hundred Years of Solitude*, along with the old book dealer.)

Also in 1950, he returned to Aracataca with his mother, in order to sell the old house. It was a young adult's return to a place that had been magical to him as a child and which he had idealized ever since. The scene made a deep impression on him, especially for the decay of what he had remembered as a grand mansion and the desolation of the hot, dusty little town. This confrontation with his childhood "made him, definitively, a writer," according to Vargas Llosa (1971:36). Apparently it was also on this trip that he became intrigued by a sign with the name of a banana farm near the town, "Macondo," the name he would give to the fictitious town of *One Hundred Years of Solitude*. (The word is the local name for a kind of shrub.)

While working for *El Heraldo* in Barranquilla, García Márquez lived in a tiny room on the top floor of a building that was basically a brothel; the whores and the pimps took a liking to him and used to visit his room to talk and ask advice, carelessly and casually giving the young writer a wealth of comic material. He also began his first attempt at a large, complex novel about his childhood, called simply *La Casa (The House)*. He finished a version of it under the new title, *La hojarasca* (literally, "Fallen Leaves," translated as Leafstorm), but his skills were not yet equal to his ambitions and he was unhappy with the book. When it was submitted to an Argentinian publisher, the book was returned with the recommendation that the author look for some other line of work (Vargas Llosa, 1971:38).

Writes "Human Interest" Stories

Nevertheless, his short stories continued to appear in the Sunday supplement of *El Espectador*, and in 1954 he returned to Bogota to work for that paper. He also wrote in this period drafts of some of the stories later included in *Los funerales de la Mama Grande* (Big Mama's Funeral). For the newspaper he specialized in human interest stories which were sometimes based on exuberant pranks or publicity stunts, closer to fiction than sober reporting, as well as a taut, beautifully crafted documentary series about a ship-wrecked sailor (which would have national repercussions when it came out that the Colombian Navy had been carrying contraband on the ship).

Wins National Fiction Award

In 1955 he won a national prize from the Asociacion de Escritores y Artistas for his story, "Un dia despues del sabado" ("One Day after Saturday"). "Isabel viendo llover en Macondo" ("Isabel Watching the Rain in Macondo"), a product of the rough draft that produced *La hojarasca*, also appeared in 1955. Then, in that same year, a publisher finally accepted the four-year old draft of *La hojarasca*, but the book was not promoted and had very poor sales.

The story, translated much later as *Leafstorm*, is set in a town named Macondo between 1903 (the end of the Conservative-Liberal "war of a thousand days") and 1928, the author's birthdate. It treats the town metaphorically, alluding to mysterious tragedies that are never clarified. As he himself has acknowledged, García Márquez at this period was heavily under the influence of the North American novelist William Faulkner (Vargas Llosa 1969:133).

Criticized By Communists - ?

According to Vargas Llosa, after this first novel appeared in 1955, García Márquez was approached by the then-illegal Communist Party of Colombia, and joined a "cell" (1971:45); García Márquez himself has insisted he was never a member of that or any other party (Dreifus 1983:67). In Vargas Llosa's version of events, "The party provided him data obtained through its underground organization which he used in his journalism. His brief membership consisted almost exclusively in political and intellectual discussions," in which he was criticized for writing in a style that was too "artistic" and inappropriate for describing Colombia's urgent problems (Vargas Llosa, 1971:45).

Whether or not García Márquez ever formally joined the Communist Party, however briefly (and, as we have pointed out, he firmly denies it), it is clear from both his writings and his later actions that he was not adapted to following anybody's party line. If there were any doubts on that point, the articles he was soon to write on Eastern Europe made it clear that, while his sympathies were with the left, he was (and is) an independent thinker who is harshly critical of any repressive system.

EUROPEAN SOJOURN

In July 1955, he left Colombia for the first time. His reports on the shipwrecked sailor had caused a scandal, because of government involvement in the smuggling on the sunken ship, and El Espectador decided to send him to Geneva to cover the "Big Four" Summit Conference. He was planning to return shortly to marry Mercedes, but the paper then cabled him to go to Rome to cover the expected death of the pope - of hiccups. The pope recovered, but García Márquez remained in Europe as the paper's correspondent. He was earning $300 a month, a very comfortable salary, and had a lot of free time. He enrolled in Rome's "Centro Sperimentale de Cinematografia," where he studied film directing for a few months and made friends with other students who would become important filmmakers.

At the end of the year he moved to Paris, but within days he learned that the dictatorship of Rojas Pinilla had closed down *El Espectador*. This cut off García Márquez's only source of income. Nevertheless, he decided to cash in his return ticket and stay in Paris to write fiction.

Starves But Writes

In Paris he lived in terrible penury. When he couldn't pay his rent, the couple who owned the building on the rue Cujas let him stay in the attic. At times he collected and resold old newspapers and bottles for a few coins, and when absolutely penniless, he might ask the butcher to lend him a bone for making soup, returning the bone the next day. Somehow he managed to write, "day and night, in a true fury," El coronel no tiene quien le escriba (No One Writes to the Colonel) - eleven times! When his typewriter broke down, the repairman shook his head and said, "Elle est fatiguee, monsieur!" ("She's tired, sir!") (Vargas Llosa 1969:135).

The old colonel of the story, like the young man who was writing it, is starving, but in the colonel's case for clearly political reasons (the government has not provided the promised pension). García Márquez's prose had also slimmed down: fewer flourishes, a terser, more direct style. He would later explain that he had "combatted" his Faulknerian influences "by reading Hemingway." He finished this "brief masterpiece," as Vargas Llosa called it, in 1957, but was not satisfied and hid it in the bottom of his suitcase, rolled up and tied with a necktie. He also worked on the typescript of what was to become *La mala hora (In Evil Hour)*.

Somehow, he scrounged up enough money (not much was needed, in any case) to travel with a pair of friends through

Eastern Europe in 1957. Magazines in Bogota and Caracas published his series of articles about these travels under the heading "90 dias en la Cortina de Hierro" ("90 Days behind the Iron Curtain"). These articles bear his signature characteristics: the use of vivid anecdotes to make his points, and a tone of taking the reader into his confidence. For example, he describes Eastern European experiences as being like or unlike things familiar to South Americans. His appreciation of the difficulties of constructing socialism in the ruins of the war is especially apparent in his article on Hungary, which he was visiting just one year after the massive and bloody anti-Soviet revolt. He details some of the gross errors the Communists had made that provoked the revolt, and considers the complexity of the problems facing Janos Kadar, the newly installed premier. Elsewhere, he is most critical of the atmosphere of gloom and stolidity in East Germany, and seems most comfortable in Czechoslovakia. At least two articles in the series foreshadow **themes** in his later fiction: In Prague, he is delighted to find a "Street of the Alchemists," preserved intact from medieval times, and in Moscow, a visit to Stalin's crypt inspires thoughts about dictatorial power.

JOURNALISM AND REVOLUTION

In October 1957 he went to London to learn English, but was there only about two months when he got word that he had been named editor of the magazine *Momento in Caracas*, Venezuela.

He arrived in Venezuela just in time to observe the death throes of the dictatorship of General Marcos Perez Jimenez, overthrown by a mass rising on January 23, 1958. Then came the return of the exiles and revelations of tortures under the old regime. García has said that this was one of the experiences that inspired his later novel about a dictator, *The Autumn of the Patriarch*.

It was in Venezuela that he finished the stories that make up his collection *Los funerales de la Mama Grande (Big Mama's Funeral)*. In March he took a quick trip back to Barranquilla, Colombia, to marry Mercedes Barcha. He also arranged to have *No One Writes to the Colonel* published in a Colombian magazine. In mid-1958, he quit *Momento* in protest when the owner insisted on making an editorial apology to Richard Nixon (then Vice President of the United States), whose car had just been stoned by angry crowds in Caracas. He spent the rest of the year working for a semipornographic scandal sheet, *Venezuela Grafica*.

In January 1959, the Cuban Revolution triumphed, and García Márquez was among its enthusiastic supporters. The revolutionary government created a news agency, Prensa Latina, to promote its slant on the news, and García Márquez and his old friend, Plinio Apuleyo Mendoza, set up an office in Bogota to report on Colombian events to Havana and also to get Colombian media to print or broadcast items from Prensa Latina - a difficult undertaking, since the press was generally hostile to the Cuban Revolution. Somehow, García Márquez also found time to write more stories and to rework his draft of what came to be called La mala hora. Also in that year, on August 24, his first son, Rodrigo, was born.

Novella Published

In 1960 he worked for *Prensa Latina* in Cuba and later in New York City, but the dogmatism of a "Stalinist" element seeking to control the agency in Havana made him fear for the independence he had to have to function as a journalist. Because he was still a supporter of the Cuban Revolution against its enemies, he waited until after the Bay of Pigs invasion (April 1961) to quit. Meanwhile, his novella about the starving colonel (*El coronel no tiene quien le escriba*) had finally been published in a small edition in Colombia.

Jobless now and almost penniless, he decided to take his family back to Colombia, first traveling by bus to New Orleans, so that he could see William Faulkner's territory and also to save money.

FREELANCE IN MEXICO: ADMAN AND SCREENWRITER

However, in New Orleans he changed plans and decided to go to Mexico to work as a screenwriter. While he was looking for work he wrote one more short story, which was to be his last fiction for years. After several weeks of a futile search for movie work, and getting deeper into debt, he accepted a job as editor of two popular magazines "on condition that he would not write even a single word in them." (Vargas Llosa 1971:67)

In April 1962 his second son, Gonzalo, was born and *Los funerales de la Mama Grande* was published in Mexico. He also entered the novel he had been working on and reworking for years in a national contest in Colombia.

He had lately been calling it *Este pueblo de mierda* (This Shitty Town), but now he was persuaded to retitle it *La mala hora* (In Evil Hour). He won the Esso prize of three thousand dollars - which he thought was undeserved (he bought a car with the money). But when the book was published in Spain, the Spanish editors had changed it so much by cleaning up the language that García Márquez disowned the book. (Later he was able to have it published the way he wanted it, and it has gone through many editions.)

He quit the magazines in 1963 and went to work for the J. Walter Thompson advertising agency. At the same time he began working on his first screenplay, in collaboration with Carlos Fuentes: *El gallo de oro*, based on a story by Juan Rulfo. (This period Gabriel García Márquez describes in "Breves nostalgias sobre Juan Rulfo," 1983.) From then on he wrote much for the screen, although few entire scripts were primarily his work (Vargas Llosa, 1971:67). In 1964 he wrote the script for *Tiempo de Morir*, a bloody story of cowboy duels and humiliations, which was later published in the Revista de Bellas Artes in Mexico. On the whole, he was not very happy with his own work as a screenwriter and much less happy with writing advertising copy. Futhermore, his whole literary vocation was in crisis, because he had not written any new fiction since 1961 and he was convinced that everything he'd written before was very poor.

BREAKTHROUGH: ONE HUNDRED YEARS OF SOLITUDE

In January 1964, as García Márquez tells the story, he was driving his Opel (which he'd bought with the Esso prize money?) on the Mexico-Acapulco highway when the whole "novela-rio" ("novel-river") came to him at once. This was the novel he had been thinking about and writing at for twenty years, the one he had thought he would call *La casa* (The House), now all suddenly falling into place. He secluded himself in his house to do nothing else but write *Cien anos de soledad* in stretches of eight to ten hours. Eighteen months after his vision, he emerged from his studio with the manuscript in hand to meet his wife

Mercedes, who was holding ten thousand dollars worth of unpaid bills.

He had sent the first three chapters to Carlos Fuentes, who was bowled over and praised them to the skies in the mass-circulation Mexican magazine, *Siempre!* More fragments then appeared in other Latin American literary journals, creating great excitement. An Argentinian publisher, *Editorial Sudamericana*, readily published *Cien anos de soledad* in 1967, and also published new editions of his earlier novels and stories. The sales were enormous, and Gabriel García Márquez could at last pay off his debts.

The prizes and critical appraisals, overwhelmingly favorable, will be discussed in detail in a later chapter. What is important here is that the amazing and sudden success transformed the life of Gabriel García Márquez. Now he could do what he had only dreamed of before: devote himself exclusively to writing what he pleased.

Fame also brought him a new problem: preserving his own solitude from reporters, politicians, and excited fans, all eager for some contact with this new literary star. He took his family to Barcelona, Spain, found a comfortable place there to write, and began work on *El otono del patriarca* (The Autumn of the Patriarch), a novel about an aged dictator. He has said that one reason for choosing Spain, then ruled by Generalissimo Francisco Franco, was that he needed to feel what it was like to live in a dictatorship. He was also becoming obsessive about his privacy. His own brother, Eligio García M., described him on a visit to his parents' house in Barcelona, Colombia, as behaving like a character in his famous novel, Colonel Aureliano Buendia, who at the height of his power has a chalk circle drawn around him and forbids anyone to enter (García M., 1982:91–98).

He had always been playful, and now that he was famous he had more opportunities to pull the legs of reporters in interviews. Among other whoppers, he told them that his novels were written by Mercedes but that he signed them because they were very bad and she didn't want the responsibility (Vargas Llosa 1971:80).

In 1969, *Cien anos de soledad* received the Chianchiana Prize in Italy and the Prix du meilleur livre etranger in France. The first English-language edition of *One Hundred Years of Solitude* appeared in 1970, and *Time* magazine named it one of the twelve best books of the year. The next year Vargas Llosa published his 664-page study of García Márquez's life and works to date, *Gabriel García Márquez: historia de un deicidio*. Then in 1972 he received Venezuela's Romulo Gallegos Prize - and scandalized the literary establishment by donating the money to the Movement Toward Socialism (MAS), a small but lively left-wing Venezuelan political party. That year he also published *Erendira*, which was written as a screenplay and was later filmed in Mexico. (This story, of a young girl forced into prostitution by her grandmother to pay a debt, had grown out of a brief scene in *Cien anos de soledad*, where the future Colonel Aureliano Buendia falls in love with a similar prostitute.) Books Abroad awarded him the Neustadt Prize that same year.

AFTER ONE HUNDRED YEARS

In 1973 he published a collection of his journalism from the 1950s, *Cuando era feliz e indocumentado*, which roughly translates, *When I Was Happy and Unknown*, alluding to his present discomfort with celebrity. As a protest against the Chilean military that had seized power in a bloody coup in September 1973, he declared that he would continue to write but not publish any more fiction until democracy was restored in that country. He has since said that he gave that answer just to get the reporters off his back and that actually he didn't have any strong fiction ideas in mind - "ran out of gasoline," he told friends - although he was working on a collection of stories (later abandoned) about Latin Americans in exile in Europe.

In 1974 he founded *Alternativa*, a leftist magazine in Bogota. The next year he relented in his vow to publish no more fiction, explaining that his Chilean friends had convinced him he should publish, because his words were more effective weapons than his silence, and published *El otono del patriarca* (The Autumn of the Patriarch), a scathing, fantastic composite portrait of all the monstrous dictators of Latin America.

In 1977 he published *Operacion Carlota*, an essay on Cuba's role in Africa, of which he approved.

In 1981 he published *Cronica de una muerte anunciada* (Chronicle of a Death Foretold), a very different kind of novel for him. It is a murder mystery where the crime and the perpetrator are known at the very beginning; the mystery is how so many decent people, knowing a murder is about to be committed, fail to take any action to prevent it.

In 1982 Gabriel García Márquez was awarded the Nobel Prize for Literature, the fourth Latin American and only the second Latin American novelist to be so honored. His acceptance speech returned to the **themes** of *One Hundred Years of Solitude*. That year, a conversation between Gabriel García Márquez and his old friend Plinio Apuleyo Mendoza, really an extended interview on García Márquez's life and writing, was published in *Colombia as El olor de la guayaba* (The Smell of the Guava).

In 1985 *El amor en los tiempos del colera* (Love in the Times of Cholera), a long novel about aged lovers, appeared (not yet translated). In 1986 he published another journalistic work, *La aventura de Miguel Littín clandestino en Chile*, about the underground adventures of the noted Chilean filmmaker, a friend who had worked with García Márquez.

THE WORD AND THE DEED

In recent years García Márquez has continued to be active in politics, both in behind-the-scenes diplomacy and as a political writer. He remains a supporter of the Cuban Revolution and other leftist causes, including the younger Nicaraguan Revolution. He considers himself a close personal friend of Cuban President Fidel Castro, with whom he says he talks mostly about literature (Castro is a voracious reader) but with whom he has also interceded privately for the release of political prisoners. He was also a close friend of General Omar Torrijos, the president of Panama who negotiated his country's recovery of the Panama Canal, and had planned to accompany the general on the plane trip in which Torrijos lost his life in 1981. Prior to the Sandinistas' 1979 triumph in Nicaragua, García Márquez "served as a secret intermediary between the Sandinistas and several governments of the region." (Riding 1983:32)

In Colombia a few years ago, a coalition of leftist parties sought him as a presidential candidate, but he declined. In 1981, while he was in Colombia shortly after a visit with Castro in Cuba, Colombian guerrillas belonging to the leftist organization M-19 landed in the southern part of the country, and García Márquez was accused of having personally coordinated the action with Castro. The accusation seems, as it seemed at the time, ridiculous; there is nothing in his career that suggests he would be very good at planning an invasion, even if he wanted to - but the government nevertheless appeared to take the notion so seriously that García fled to the protection of the Mexican embassy. His relationship with the Colombian government improved with the election of President Belisario Betancur (ironically, a Conservative), who offered him an ambassadorship. The author declined, preferring what he calls "secret diplomacy." He has said, "If I were not a Latin American, I would not be in politics. But how can the intellectual enjoy the luxury of debating the destiny of the soul when the problems are of physical survival, health, education, ignorance and so on?" (Riding 1983:32)

His Books Banned In Chile

He also has continued to write about politics in the book about Littin and in articles on the assassination of Chile's President Salvador Allende, Cuba's presence in Africa, the Sandinista Revolution, and so on, and, in much subtler ways, through the values he expresses in his fiction. General Augusto Pinochet of Chile considers his words so dangerous that in 1987 he ordered the confiscation and destruction of a shipload of García Márquez's books. The United States State Department evidently regards his words as dangerous as well, since he continues to be refused a visa for unrestricted multiple entries into the United States; having been declared "ineligible for entry," he must apply for a conditional visa each time he is invited to lecture or wishes to consult with colleagues in this country.

Does García Márquez truly believe he "would have been more useful to humanity" as a "terrorist" than as a writer, as he said in the passage quoted at the beginning of this chapter?

We know from his life and his works that he is a lover of **irony** who often uses wild exaggeration to make a point - but that there usually is a point. We also know that he is appalled by senseless violence, so he could only have been using the word "terrorist" ironically, as his opponents would use it, for someone who takes up arms against the oppression symbolized by the police.

In sum, Gabriel García Márquez is a man of the left who believes, as he has often said, that revolution - and therefore, revolutionary violence - is necessary to end the institutionalized violence of dictatorial regimes, capitalist exploitation, and retarded development in the poorer countries of the world. But, whether he personally is convinced of this or not, both his enemies and his supporters would agree that he has done more for the cause he believes in with his typewriter than he could ever have accomplished with a machine gun.

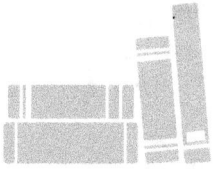

INTRODUCTION TO ONE HUNDRED YEARS OF SOLITUDE

HIS PLACE IN LATIN AMERICAN AND WORLD LITERATURE

In 1967, after the manuscript had been turned down by publishers in Spain and Mexico, the Editorial Sudamericana in Buenos Aires took the risk of publishing the fourth novel of an obscure Colombian journalist and screenwriter, Gabriel García Márquez. To everyone's amazement, including the author's, *Cien anos de soledad* instantly became a runaway best seller, one of the biggest in Latin American publishing history. It was not only a popular success, it also drew rave reviews from critics, including some of the biggest names in Spanish-language fiction, like Carlos Fuentes (Mexico) and Julio Cortazar (Argentina, but living in France). By 1976, Sudamericana had sold over two million copies in forty-six printings (and had also done well on new editions of García Márquez's earlier books). Large, simultaneous editions in Barcelona, Madrid, Havana, and Bogota also sold out. García Márquez became such a celebrity that, for the first time in his life, he had to hide from reporters - and, also for the first time in his life, could support himself solely by writing fiction. The book was also an enormous success abroad, and has been translated into at least twenty-four languages, including Farsi, Croatian, Russian, German, French, Japanese, and (in 1970) English, in which it is entitled *One Hundred Years of Solitude*.

The main reasons for the success and continued popularity of *One Hundred Years of Solitude* are that it is a joy to read, full of wonderfully quirky characters, rollicking sex, dramatic violence, and high comedy - plus all the special traits listed at the end of this section. But there were also certain historical developments, literary, social, and political, that contributed to the book's powerful impact from the day it was published.

ONE HUNDRED YEARS AND THE "BOOM"

One Hundred Years of Solitude appeared in the midst of the 1960s "boom" of Latin American fiction, so-called because it was truly an explosion of talent. Young writers all over Latin America were experimenting with new **themes** and new forms of expression, and found a ready audience among university students, young professionals, and even some of the more educated workers. Carlos Fuentes (Mexico), Jose Donoso (Chile), Julio Cortazar (Argentina), Mario Vargas Llosa (Peru), and Juan Rulfo (Mexico) were just a few of the better-known writers whose work appeared in low-priced, popular editions and in the new literary journals that sprang up in every city that had a university.

Part of the explanation for the boom is literary, the maturing of certain traditions in Latin American fiction and poetry. The young authors had absorbed the lessons of an older generation of Latin American writers - Pablo Neruda, Jorge Luis Borges, Cesar Vallejo, Alejo Carpentier, Romulo Gallegos, Miguel Angel Asturias, and others, from an earlier "boom" of the 1920s and 1930s. They had also been influenced by translations of world literature, especially works in English, "from Sterne to Faulkner by way of Dos Passos and Joyce," as one observer has put it (Janes, 1981:4), and were ready to experiment with new styles.

A second part of the explanation for the boom of the 1960s is social. A very large cohort of Latin Americans, better educated than their predecessors, was coming of age in the 1960s (Latin America had also experienced a baby boom), and was receptive to writing that expressed their own youthful rebelliousness. Thus, there was a much larger audience for these works than there had been in the 1940s and 1950s.

Another social factor was the substantive impact of film and television, which prepared both writers and readers for faster-paced stories, jump cuts, and other stylistic experiments.

Cuban Revolution

But these factors alone do not explain the special character and importance of the boom. What stimulated their audience and brought the writers themselves together in a common purpose was, more than anything else, a political event: the Cuban Revolution.

In the two decades between the collapse of the Latin American revolutionary movements of the late 1920s and 1930s (Sandino in Nicaragua, the overthrow of Machado in Cuba, coups and strikes in Argentina and Chile, and so on) and the 1959 triumphal march of Fidel Castro into Havana, Latin American fiction and poetry had become pessimistic and hermetic, that is, written without hope of a wide audience. The more openly political writers (e.g., Miguel Angel Asturias and Alejo Carpentier) raged against their countries' impotence to solve social problems, which was rather depressing. Others, such as Borges or Guillermo Meneses, either avoided social and political issues or alluded to them indirectly, in an exquisite surrealistic style that was not intended for the masses.

The crushing problems of Latin America were obvious to everyone: sweeping social inequalities, lack of an infrastructure of schools, hospitals, even roads, the draining of national wealth by local elites and foreign corporations, with savage police and military establishments protecting the whole rotten system. For generations, intellectuals who criticized the abuses were targeted for death or imprisonment by their regimes. The poet Neruda had been chased through the forests of southern Chile by police, the novelist Romulo Gallegos had been exiled from Venezuela by a military junta, journalist Julio Antonio Mella had been shot down on a Mexican street by agents of the Cuban dictator Machado, and thousands of lesser known intellectuals and university students had suffered imprisonment, torture, and death.

The Cuban Revolution promised the end of political impotence and the liberation of social criticism. Here, at last, a Latin American people had thrown out their dictator and embarked on fundamental structural reforms. Not only that, the new revolutionary government even stood up to the government of the United States, which had traditionally been the final guarantor of conservative regimes in Latin America.

The early enthusiasm for the Cuban Revolution among the young intellectuals of Latin America cannot be overstated. It was not to last: transformations within Cuba, a changing international situation, and the aging of the intellectuals themselves would all contribute to a considerable cooling toward Cuban socialism, especially after the Cubans jailed the poet Heberto Padilla, in 1971, for reasons that are still controversial. But in the early years, the choice was clear: you were either for Cuba, or you were for military dictatorship, poverty, and foreign exploitation. And if the Cubans could make a revolution, the other Latin Americans believed, so could they.

Impact On Writers

The effects of the Cuban revolution on literature included a liberation of the imagination - because all things seemed possible - and a renewed interest in the region's social problems. Serious fiction could now be joyous and optimistic, and still talk about politics. The Cubans also took several specific, concrete steps that spurred the boom: first and most important, they carried out the most successful literacy campaign in history, thus dramatically increasing the size of the reading public in their own country and setting a standard for other countries; second, they established a new publishing house, Casa de las Americas, which sponsored contests for new novels from anywhere in Latin America and distributed them in large, inexpensive editions, and finally, they opened their own new cultural journals to leftist and experimental writers.

The boom also benefited writers whose main work had been done before the Cuban Revolution, like the Mexican Juan Rulfo, who found a new audience for his **themes** of rural poverty and violence. Since there were now so many writers with similar concerns, a subculture was created that helped new writers, both morally and pragmatically. They promoted one another's writings through reviews in journals, they traded information on the best places to stay when in exile in Paris or Barcelona, they helped one another make contacts with publishers, because they saw themselves as allies against the elitist and repressed literature of the past. García Márquez was one of the beneficiaries of this literary comradeship, in which competition for the most part was still friendly. Thus, it was natural that other important Latin American novelists praised and promoted his magnificent novel.

Having benefited from the preexisting boom, *One Hundred Years of Solitude* also gave it a big boost. Its immense popularity in Latin America led to translations in other languages, and it proved to be so popular abroad that it won new audiences for Latin American literature in Europe and the United States. This, in turn, has made it easier for publishers to sell books by Manuel Puig (Argentina), Mario Vargas Llosa (Peru), and many others.

ONE HUNDRED YEARS AND WORLD LITERATURE

At the time *One Hundred Years of Solitude* appeared, critics in Europe and North America had been mourning what was called "the death of the novel." Modernism, as represented by William Faulkner, James Joyce, John Dos Passos, and other experimental writers of the 1920s through the 1950s, had exhausted (so they believed) all the possibilities of saying anything interesting or new about the world. Novels were still being written, of course, but they were considered (by these critics) "dead" at the soul, mere repetitions of exhausted formulas. For interesting writing, it was believed, one had to look to nonfiction, or perhaps to poetry.

But then García Márquez burst onto the scene, followed closely by all these other Latin American storytellers. The material was fresh, and that alone made the stories interesting. But beyond that, García Márquez had absorbed the lessons of Dos Passos, Hemingway, Faulkner, Virginia Woolf, James Joyce, and the other great innovators in English-language literature, as well the great Spanish writers, finding new possibilities of expression that amazed foreign audiences. They were particularly impressed by his easy-flowing blend of fantasy and **realism**, his ability to treat completely fantastic and impossible events in the same straight-faced style used to report the heat and dust of a little town. The technique, quickly labeled "magic **realism**" or "the marvelous real," allowed dreamlike (or nightmarish) experiences to comment on and enhance more down-to-earth events.

With this novel, Latin American fiction was no longer trying to catch up to the world literary vanguard. It had become the vanguard. García Márquez's work has suggested to writers everywhere ways to shake loose their conceptions of time and their notions of the boundaries between the real and the imaginary. Contemporary writers from Milan Kundera (Czechoslovakia) to Robert Coover (United States) have, at the least, felt strengthened in their own experimentation by reading García Márquez.

REASONS FOR FAME

The book, besides being very funny and full of fast-moving anecdotes, has several specific traits that have been praised by readers and literary critics repeatedly.

1. The novel summarizes some four centuries of Latin American history in a simplified but powerful way: Spanish conquest and pioneer settlements, devastating pirate raids, civil wars, the introduction of technology and urban institutions (police, prostitution, bureaucracy), exploitation and domination by North American capitalists, labor protests and defeat, until

finally the whole traditional way of life is blown away (in *One Hundred Years of Solitude*, literally blown away). The only major events omitted from this historical fable, curiously, are the wars of independence (1810 to about 1820).

2. Utterly fantastic events (a gypsy returns from the dead, a girl ascends to heaven, a priest levitates, a man is surrounded by yellow butterflies, and so on) are told with a perfectly straight face, recalling our own childhood naivete when such things seemed possible and necessary. The effect is especially strong on Latin American readers, who are likely to have experienced versions of these very same myths in their own childhoods, and who can therefore delight in remembering that lost innocence.

3. Other funny or grotesque events and situations from small-town life are not fantastic at all (although they may be somewhat exaggerated) and bring a smile of recognition to readers in Latin America and probably other areas where traditional ways of life survive. For example, it is not at all implausible in Latin America for a military leader to have had numerous children by several different women, although probably not by seventeen different women and probably not all male children, as is the case with Colonel Aureliano Buendia.

4. The pain of some of the terrible violence in the book is made bearable by the author's focus on those few characters who, however damaged, survive to carry on their struggle and pass it on to the next generation.

5. Related to the traits mentioned in items 3 and 4, is the author's enormous sympathy for his characters, even when they behave foolishly or destructively. He makes us care what happens to them. Almost every character who is given a name and a face is treated sympathetically. Except for Mr. Brown, the banana entrepreneur, and General Carlos Cortes Vargas, commander in the massacre of banana workers, the evildoers are nameless as well as faceless, as though the author did not want to waste his or the reader's attention on such people (the black-suited lawyers who hover around like vultures, the anonymous troops of Cortes Vargas, the police who shoot down Colonel Aureliano Buendia's seventeen sons).

6. The book is intellectually engaging, giving hints and foretastes of what is to come and throwing out clues along the way as to its intricate structure.

7. *One Hundred Years of Solitude* is very flattering to the reader, who always understands much more of what is going on than do the characters themselves - as though the author and reader shared a big secret. This is sometimes because the characters are too naive to understand their own behavior (e.g., Fernanda) or because vital information has been inaccessible to them (e.g., the last of the Aurelianos), but also because of the clues mentioned in item 6 (the structure that the characters do not perceive).

8. The structure of the book is a kind of spiral, in which similar events recur but never quite the same way. The whole story, then, is spiraling toward an inexorable

conclusion. Thus the end, when it comes, seems inevitable, and the book achieves a satisfying closure.

9. It can be enjoyed at many levels, offering new rewards on a second and third reading. The anecdotes are entertaining in themselves, the sex is exciting and the dialogue amusing, which is quite enough for an enjoyable first reading. In addition, however, all these anecdotes are linked to a general scheme that gives the whole story coherence. On yet another level, the repetition of the same kinds of events, and the remarks of several of the characters, suggest certain philosophical views about human nature, the corrupting influence of power, the meaning of love and solitude, the nature of literature itself, and many other things.

10. At one of the levels mentioned in item 9, the book has been a special delight to professors and critics of literature: it is a very clever, good-natured literary spoof. For one thing, there are literary in-jokes. Those in the know will recognize at least two characters lifted right out of works by other novelists (Julio Cortazar and Carlos Fuentes among them) and given minor roles in *One Hundred Years*. The author himself, several friends from his youth and his wife also appear, under their own names, in the final chapters. But besides these inside jokes, the author also satirizes literature itself, for example by making one character, a Catalan bookdealer, declare that "literature is the best toy ever invented to make fun of people." Most intriguing is that a close rereading will reveal many comments on the creation of the very book we are reading, disguised as observations about the characters.

The Nobel Prize

In 1982, when Gabriel García Márquez was awarded the Nobel Prize for Literature, it was primarily in recognition of his accomplishment in *One Hundred Years of Solitude*, which had come to symbolize all that was new and vibrant in Latin American literature. Today it is probably the most widely known and widely read novel by any living writer in Spanish.

A NOTE ON NAMES

For those unfamiliar with Spanish pronunciation, the author's name is pronounced (approximately) ga-bree-El gar-See-ah Mar-kess.

Like many Spanish speakers, the author uses a double surname, adding his mother's maiden name, Márquez, after his father's surname, García. Thus, instead of calling himself "Gabriel García, Jr.," the novelist has become "Gabriel García Márquez." People with very common surnames are especially likely to distinguish themselves this way. (As an indication of how common the name is, the New York University Library holds titles by 255 authors named García and by 21 others named Márquez, with or without a second surname.)

Common as it is, García, not Márquez, is the name he passes on to his own sons and that he himself might be called for short; many English speakers do not understand this practice, and so they mistakenly refer to the author as "Márquez," thinking the last name must be the more important one. It is not; for instance, the author's younger brother, also a writer, signs himself simply "Eligio García M."

When referring to the author in a study, review, and so on, it is best to use the full double surname, García Márquez, at least for the first reference (this is the way his works will be cataloged in libraries, indexes, and so on); thereafter, if that seems tiresome, one may use "García" alone or, as many critics do, write "GM" or "GGM."

The same principle applies, incidentally, to other double surnames in Spanish: Mario Vargas Llosa, Guillermo Cabrera Infante, Miguel de Cervantes Saavedra, Fidel Castro Ruz.

TRANSLATION COMPARED TO ORIGINAL

Gregory Rabassa's translation of *One Hundred Years of Solitude* (New York: Avon Books, 1971) is fluent, vigorous, and almost always very close to the sense of the original; García Márquez himself, in a very gracious hyperbole, has even said he liked the English translation better than the original (McDowell, 1986:36). Nevertheless, it is a translation, and some nuances are inevitably lost. These include such minor literary effects as puns and other wordplay, **alliteration**, and onomatopoeia (use of words that sound like the thing they name), all of which are frequent in the original and almost impossible to reproduce in another language. The losses also include the **connotations** of certain Latin American terms and practices, a problem not merely of translation but of the foreign reader's ignorance of the Latin American culture; for example, Rabassa, not wishing to confuse the reader, translates "compadre" to the much blander word, "friend," which weakens the **irony** in a crucial dialogue in the eighth chapter. In this Note, prepared from the Spanish text, such nuances will be pointed out and the cultural background explained; thus an English speaker who reads the translation plus this Note will be at less of a disadvantage than someone reading the novel in Spanish.

Quotations from *One Hundred Years of Solitude* used in this study have been taken from the scholarly edition of *Cien anos de soledad* prepared by Jacques Joset (Madrid: Ediciones Catedra, S.A., 1984). Translations are by this author, Geoffrey Fox, and may vary slightly from those in *One Hundred Years of Solitude* as translated by Gregory Rabassa. For the convenience of students, page numbers from the Joset edition are followed by those for the corresponding passages in the Rabassa translation.

ONE HUNDRED YEARS OF SOLITUDE

OVERVIEW

One Hundred Years of Solitude is a tall tale, in which comical exaggerations alternate with descriptions of real events that sometimes seem even more fantastic. It is ostensibly the history of the town of Macondo and of several generations of the town's leading family, the Buendias, but its real **themes** are vast, alluding to the whole social history of Latin America and to the very basis of social coexistence. We shall first summarize the story; then we shall discuss the **themes** and, finally, the structure and techniques.

The novel contains scores of characters with individual, yet interwoven, stories. Because of the complexity of stories and themes, and because of the long-time span covered (about 140, not just 100 years), the book gives the impression of being much larger than its 350 or so pages (depending on the edition; the English translation runs about 30 pages long). It is impossible to summarize or even mention all the characters and events in the space available here for a synopsis.

Instead, what follows is an extremely simplified, schematic version of the chief events in the history of the town of Macondo and in the lives of a few of the Buendias, the absolute minimum for a critical discussion. It is no substitute for reading the story as García Márquez wrote it. It is intended that, by reading this Note in conjunction with the novel itself, the English-speaking reader will catch more of the subtleties and implications of García Márquez's text, so as to enjoy a literary experience nearly as rich as that of a reader from García Márquez's native Colombia. Following the schematic summary, in this same chapter, is a discussion of the **themes** and techniques of the book. Chapter IV will analyze each chapter, and fuller discussions of the characters and character types will be found in chapter V.

HISTORY OF MACONDO

Primitive Settlement And First Contacts With The Outside

In the early nineteenth century, Jose Arcadio Buendia leads twenty-two families to found Macondo, an isolated agricultural village of mud and wattle houses in the wilderness. The Macondinos (people of Macondo) become aware of discoveries and inventions from the outside world when Melquiades, a wandering gypsy magician, introduce, magnets, a magnifying glass, alchemists' lore, and so on. He amazes the villagers, especially Buendia, who pursues extravagant experiments and neglects his duties to family and village. Buendia also tries, but fails, to find a route to the outside.

His wife, Ursula Iguaran, brings strangers to Macondo, which begins to develop into a small commercial town. Buendia finally goes mad from his frenzied attempts to comprehend all the changes, and is tied to a chestnut tree in the patio, where he eventually dies. Melquiades, meanwhile, has returned to live in the Buendia house and write a long document in a strange script. He dies, but his spirit will return occasionally to coach those who try to decipher his manuscripts.

The Civil Wars

Because Ursula is her husband's cousin, she had feared giving birth to a child with a pig's tail, but her children are normal. The eldest, Jose Arcadio, grows to be a huge, powerful, and aggressive man who, after adventures abroad, returns to Macondo to become the town's biggest landowner. The second son, more meditative and solitary, becomes the powerful Colonel Aureliano Buendia, a leader of the Liberals in thirty-two civil wars. Macondo suffers alternative occupations by Conservative and Liberal troops, with varying degrees of brutality and tyranny. Originally, the Liberals are economic reformers and freethinkers, whereas the Conservatives defend their privileges as wealthy oligarchs and use the Church to enforce ideological conformity. Accordingly, the colonel redistributes the lands his older brother has more or less stolen from his neighbors. In the course of the wars, however, the colonel grows bitter and cynical, losing sight of his cause but continuing to fight "out of pride." After his surrender and failed suicide attempt, he settles in his old room to make and unmake little goldfishes until at last he dies, unbearably lonely.

Amaranta, the Buendias' daughter, meanwhile sabotages her foster sister Rebeca's romance with a newcomer to Macondo, Pietro Crespi, by a series of dirty tricks. Rebeca then goes off to live with Jose Arcadio and Crespi decides to woo Amaranta instead, but Amaranta spurns him. She will continue to entice men sexually only to turn them away when they begin to get serious, and will finally die a virgin.

The colonel's many illegitimate sons (seventeen engendered during the war and one by Macondo's fortuneteller, Pilar Ternera) will all die violently without leaving offspring. The Buendia bloodline is carried on by descendants of the colonel's brother, Jose Arcadio (who is mysteriously murdered), through his illegitimate son by the same Pilar Ternera.

The Banana Company And Worker Protest

After the civil wars, Macondo is tranquil and modestly prosperous. It acquires a police department and a movie theatre. Then a North American, Mr. Brown, establishes a banana plantation nearby. The company attracts workers from all over the country and the Caribbean, builds a fenced-in residential area for the North American families, and brings a period of frenzied wealth and dissipation. Jose Arcadio Segundo ("the Second"), a great-grandson of Macondo's founder, becomes an organizer of the banana workers, who go on strike to demand improvements in the atrocious working conditions. Three thousand strikers are massacred by troops when they assemble for a protest. Jose Arcadio Segundo is the sole survivor, and his shock and the refusal of the townspeople to believe the massacre took place drive him mad. He secludes himself in Melquiades's old room, trying to decipher the manuscripts. He will leave no children.

The Decay Of Macondo

Jose Arcadio Segundo's twin brother, Aureliano Segundo, a wealthy, pleasure-loving cattleman, has two daughters and a son by his wife, the grim Fernanda del Carpio. When Fernanda discovers that a banana company peon, Mauricio Babilonia, is secretly visiting her elder daughter, Meme, she causes him to be shot and hustles her traumatized daughter off to a distant nunnery. A nun brings back Meme's baby, Aureliano, whom Fernanda tries to hide. The boy grows up without leaving the house and studies Melquiades's manuscripts, also learning much from his great-uncle, the mad Jose Arcadio Segundo.

Heavy, continuous rains, caused by Mr. Brown in order to evade fulfillment of the banana company's agreements, fall on Macondo for nearly five years. The rains ruin the town, destroying livestock and crops and washing away streets and parts of houses. When the rains finally stop, Ursula tries to restore the old house but it is too much for her and, ancient and senile, she dies. Aureliano Segundo and his longtime mistress, Petra Cotes, try to recover their former wealth by raffling the few surviving animals.

Love At Last, Insight And Destruction

Fernanda and Aureliano Segundo's second daughter, Amaranta Ursula, who has been the younger Aureliano's only playmate, is sent off Belgium to study, and the son, Jose Arcadio, goes to Rome to train to become pope. After the deaths of his parents, Jose Arcadio (who hasn't studied anything) returns to Macondo expecting to find a promised inheritance, but all he finds is decay; he plays sexual games with young boys until, to avenge a beating, they kill him.

Aureliano, instructed by Melquiades's ghost, discovers a bookstore of wonderful, rare volumes, as well as the local brothels, where he amazes the women by his extraordinary virility. Amaranta Ursula returns with a Belgian husband and tries to restore the house, battling the ants and termites. Aureliano falls desperately in love with her and finally half-rapes, half-seduces her. They become lovers (the Belgian, bored in Macondo, returns to Europe) and, ignorant of their relationship (Amaranta Ursula is Aureliano's aunt), are delighted when she becomes pregnant.

She gives birth to a large, healthy boy with a pig's tail, the first Buendia engendered in love. But then she hemorrhages to death. Aureliano, wild with grief, wanders the town drunkenly until he suddenly remembers the baby and rushes back. He finds the baby's carcass being carried off by the ants that have been eating away at the house ever since the rains.

Aureliano seizes Melquiades's manuscripts, suddenly understanding their epigraph: "The first of the line is tied to a tree and the last is being eaten by ants." He reads the whole history of Macondo and the Buendias, skipping ahead to read of his own death and the destruction of Macondo just as a hurricane sweeps away what remains of the town, and understands at last that "the bloodlines condemned to one hundred years of solitude do not have a second opportunity on earth."

THEMES: HISTORICAL

García Márquez has said that *"One Hundred Years of Solitude* is not a history of Latin America, it is a **metaphor** for Latin America." (Dreifus 1983:1974) The historical **themes** include; conquest and colonization, settlement and scientific discovery, civil wars, foreign economic intervention, technological change, and finally the decay and disappearance of a long-established way of life.

The original Spanish conquest is alluded to when, in the first chapter, Jose Arcadio Buendia finds an old suit of armor and the remains of a galleon, mysteriously stranded several kilometers from the sea. The early Spanish colonization and the devastating pirate raids of the English sailor, Sir Francis Drake, are referred to in the second chapter. Subsequently, no more is made of this theme.

Pioneer settlement is the real beginning of the story of Macondo. It is at first "a village of twenty houses of mud and canestalks on the bank of a diaphanous river... . The world was so new, many things did not have names, and to mention them one had to point with a finger." (71) Just so: when the real pioneer families made their first crude homes in the forests of the Americas, they found many things-plants, animals, minerals - they had never seen before and for which they had no names. That was one reason Europeans referred to the western hemisphere lands as the New World. Typical of such villages, which were established on the banks of rivers in all the Spanish territories, Macondo is governed by its founder, Jose Arcadio Buendia, as a kind of village chief; Ursula, his wife, cultivates a little plot of land and the men, apparently, also hunt for food (although hunting is not specifically mentioned until much later). The village, then, is poor but self-sufficient. (To maintain the rigorous logic of the narrative, there should be twenty-two houses in the first settlement, since Jose Arcadio Buendia led twenty-one families, plus his own, in the founding. Twenty was probably chosen in this instance because García Márquez wanted a smooth, flowing rhythm in his opening lines, which would have been disrupted by an extra syllable: veintidos instead of veinte.)

An important omission from García Márquez's metaphorical history of Latin America is the savagely cruel wars for independence, which last from 1810 to (in Colombia) 1819. We can assume then that these wars are already over by the time Macondo is founded, so that this fictional act corresponds to developments in about 1820 – 1825 in the country's real history. This primitive stage of Macondo is also a time of innocence, a psychological theme important in the book.

The arrival of Melquiades and his gypsy band, with their navigational instruments, magnifying glass, and so forth, is a **metaphor** for the beginning of technical and scientific awareness, which would have reached towns like Macondo sometime between 1830 and 1860. In real history, the bearers of this new knowledge would probably not have been gypsies but itinerant professors and self-proclaimed physicians (such a quack does show up in Macondo, a disguised terrorist madman who tries to spur the youth to violence).

Effect Of Power On Idealism

The thirty-two armed rebellions fought and lost by Colonel Aureliano Buendia are clearly a **metaphor** for the wars fought by the author's real grandfather, Colonel Nicolas Márquez, at the turn of the century, especially the War of a Thousand Days (1899–1902). The fictional colonel combines characteristics of Colonel Márquez and of the commander of Liberal forces in the region, General Rafael Uribe Uribe. But the fictional colonel represents much more than just this specific historical event, or these two historical people.

The career of Colonel Aureliano Buendia is a study of the corrupting effects of violence and power on idealism. He begins as an idealist, leading an uprising against the Conservatives because he is repelled by their injustice. In the early years of his fighting, he is generous and humane toward his enemies and very strict in bringing about land reform, even when it affects his family's property. But he becomes increasingly cynical as the fighting goes on and on with no end in sight, and as the political leaders of the Liberals sell out in deals what the colonel has won on the battlefield. Finally he is fighting "out of pride," he says, or out of sheer inability to surrender the great power he holds over those around him. When that power is threatened by a rival Liberal army chief, he hints to his followers that he'd like the rival killed; when that wish is fulfilled, the colonel then orders the death of the young man who had been the murderer.

Reflections Of Stalinism

The colonel also becomes extremely isolated in his power. Women come to him in the night because they want to bear the children of this famous man, and he makes love without loving them, never even waiting until daylight to see their faces. He has his aides draw a chalk circle around him, and forbids anyone, even his mother, to enter the circle. Of course, at the end he gives up his power - when he surrenders and goes back to the old house - but he never gives up his isolation. This is a historical **theme** that partly reflects García Márquez's meditations on Joseph Stalin (see chapter II, page 23) as well as on the many dictators of Latin America. It is the **theme** of the corruption by political power generally.

After the wars, Yankee capitalism arrives. In real history, the United Fruit Company began operations near the García hometown of Aracataca in 1908, and did actually transform it, in much the way the novel describes. Prostitution flourished; some people became so rich they were said to have burned banknotes at wild parties with nude dancers; a fenced-off enclave was built for a North American town-within-a-town; and the company paid off the police and the judges in order to get away with anything it pleased. The strike in the novel actually took place, starting in 1928, and the strikers actually were shot down at a meeting in a railroad station the following year. The novel even uses the real name and real words of the commanding general. What is fictional is the presence of Jose Arcadio Segundo and of Lorenzo Gavilan, who is actually a character from Carlos Fuentes' novel, *The Death of Artemio Cruz*. (In Artemio, Fuentes seemed to have forgotten about this character from the Mexican Revolution and never resolved what happened to him; therefore García Márquez finished the story by having him migrate to Colombia to organize banana workers.) The other fictional element is the gross exaggeration of the numbers of dead: three thousand. At that time, there were probably not three thousand people in the whole town of Aracataca.

Banana Company Symbolic

Although closely based on a particular real event, the story of the banana company in Macondo represents a general phenomenon, the violent clashes between workers and troops in the pay of foreign capitalists throughout Latin America.

After the departure of the banana company, everything in the town seems to decay very rapidly. In real history, this is the period of the worldwide economic depression that began in 1929 and lasted a decade, until the beginning of World War II.

Then, in the last chapter, when the last Aureliano finally leaves the house that has been his prison, we seem to be in a new kind of Macondo. There are more people around, including several who are quite unlike any we've met before and seem unrelated to the old families of Macondo. What sort of town is this that has an eccentric Catalan dealer in rare books frequented by a group of eager young writers? The town also has a drugstore, which we have never heard about before, attended by an Egyptian-eyed girl named Mercedes. It also has some new and extravagant brothels.

Life After Macondo

The Macondo of this period seems not to be based on the author's memories of Aracataca but rather of his later memories of the city of Barranquilla, where he hung out with writers with the same names as these young men and with an older Catalan writer, Ramon Vinyes, who had once been a book dealer, courted a girl named Mercedes, and spent a lot of time with prostitutes. The two places get mixed together in this chapter, because through characters like Gabriel he is suggesting that there is a life after Macondo; while through Aureliano, who stays in the old house to the bitter end, he portrays the utter destruction of the town and family.

In real history, what was destroyed? The town of Aracataca still exists, though it doesn't amount to much. Its old way of life, its customs, perhaps even its memory of its own past, may have been swept away, or at least, this is what García Márquez seems to have felt. Perhaps what was really destroyed was the magical hold this past had over Gabriel García Márquez's imagination. He had freed himself from a twenty-year obsession to write the full story of Macondo. The only way to do that, once he got to the end, was to destroy the mythical town.

THEMES: PHILOSOPHICAL AND PSYCHOLOGICAL

SOLITUDE, SOLIDARITY, AND SEXUALITY

Soledad in Spanish means more than our word "solitude," although it means that too. It suggests loneliness, the sense of being apart from others. Although ultimately each human being is alone, because there are parts of our experience we cannot share, some people are more solitary than others. The really solitary figures in this novel are those who deliberately cut themselves off from other humans. They are contrasted with characters who combat their solitude, by making strenuous efforts to reach out to others.

The founder of Macondo, Jose Arcadio Buendia, is the first great solitary. He becomes so obsessed with his own search for truth that he neglects his family and ultimately loses all touch with outer reality. His wife, Ursula, is perhaps the greatest of the antisolitary figures, the person who more than anyone else holds the family and the house together. She takes in a foster child and later insists on rearing the bastard children of her sons and grandsons. Her whole life is devoted to strengthening social bonds.

Pilar Ternera, the fortuneteller, is also an antisolitary. Her role is to comfort the Buendia men and, in her younger years, to go to bed with them and bear their children. At the end of the book and of her very own long life (she has stopped counting birthdays after one-hundred forty-five), she is the madame of a wonderful zoological brothel, which in this context stands for a generous, bountiful sexuality.

There is a lot of sex in the novel, most of it celebrating the size and potency of the Buendia men's phalluses or the lubricity of the women. Sex can be used to combat solitude, because of its power to connect one person to another. Even the two rapes in the novel result in close bonding: Jose Arcadio Buendia rapes his bride Ursula to begin the family line (second chapter), and the last Aureliano rapes Amaranta Ursula (who is not, however, very resistant), who will bring forth the last of the line. However, for sex to really work against solitude, it must be joyful, loving sex. The colonel, after all, has had lots of women, but he doesn't remember any of them (except perhaps his deceased child bride) and shows no affection toward his bastard sons. He is never depicted as cruel sexually, simply indifferent. And thus he is condemned to loneliness.

Power Without Love

Colonel Aureliano Buendia cannot love and so, despite his power over others, he is utterly alone. The futility and desperation of his solitude is proven partly by his frustrated suicide attempt, and then even more obviously by his constant making and unmaking of little goldfishes, just to keep himself from thinking about his condition. His sister Amaranta is another great and tragic solitary. She is offered love, and seems tempted to accept it, but always turns it down. Self-punishment is part of the discipline of the solitary. Amaranta punishes herself not only by denying herself love, but also by deliberately holding her hand in a flame until she is permanently injured.

All the Buendia men, and most of the women, seem to have a vocation for solitude. The last man and woman of the line, Aureliano and Amaranta Ursula, are truly in love, and their baby is the first in the history of the family to be engendered in love. The author seems to be saying that this, love, is the great antidote to solitude. But it is too late for this family. Even though the baby is healthy and seems capable of prolonging the family line, he cannot survive, because a family condemned to a hundred years of solitude has only one chance on earth.

LITERARY TECHNIQUES AND THE STRUCTURE OF THE BOOK

Even this brief treatment, which leaves out numerous subplots involving dozens of characters, gives some idea of the enormous complexity and scope of the novel. As discussed in chapter II, on García Márquez's life and career, it took the author twenty years of constant writing and reading to perfect the devices that enable him to tie all these elements together. It is an intricately plotted book, all the **episodes** echoing and reinforcing one another so that, at the end, it is the entire book rather than just the conclusion that hits the reader with full force. It is for its complexity and its exceptional coherence that the Peruvian novelist Mario Vargas Llosa called it a "total novel."

Conscious And Unconscious Symbolism

García Márquez's writing is very rich in allusions. A character's name, an object, or an event may bring to the reader's mind connections with other events in the novel or the world, or with philosophical or psychological issues, or with all of these simultaneously. When an image or an event alludes to or represents something else, we say it is a symbol of that other thing.

Symbolism, for purposes of this discussion, is the use of an image or an event to represent a larger **theme** of the novel. It should be noted that symbolism is not necessarily conscious or deliberate on the part of an author, but this does not make it any less real. In many cases, García Márquez's selection of a particular image may be completely intuitive, that is, spontaneous or unplanned. For example, Remedios the beautiful ascends to heaven when she goes out to hang up sheets. This anecdote appears to be a version of a story García Márquez heard as a boy about a girl in his hometown (see chapter II of this Note). Still, it will remind readers of the popular legend (not to be found in the Bible, but believed by many Christians) of Mary's bodily ascension, and suggests a gentle joke at the expense of the extremely devout. The anecdote, along with the description of Remedios's character, also symbolizes absolute purity of spirit, and thus heightens the effect of the vulgarity and lust of the men around her and the hollowness of her sister-in-law Fernanda's piety.

It is easy to go overboard in discovering symbols where they were not intended. Nevertheless, the same authorial mind that developed the **themes** also fashioned the images; discussing symbolism is a way of discovering the connections between the two. More of these connections will be pointed out in the chapter-by-chapter analysis in chapter IV of this Note. Perceiving them will help the student understand the **themes** and the artistic coherence of the book.

Flashbacks And Flashforwards

One pair of devices García Márquez uses extremely skillfully is flashbacks and flashforwards. Flashbacks are references to events prior to the novel's present time. These are fairly common in literature; often a novelist will interrupt the story to tell you about the hero's earlier life, for example.

Flashforwards, anticipations of events that will occur later on in the novel, are less common. A writer may give the reader a hint of some looming threat or other event, sometimes called **foreshadowing**, but will rarely describe the details of the coming event, because that might rob the story of its suspense. In *One Hundred Years of Solitude*, however, vivid images of things that have not yet happened are used in ways that keep you reading. Furthermore, to create the particular impression of time that he wants to convey, the author may even use a flashback and flashforward in the same passage.

The best, and most famous, example is in the first two sentences of the novel:

> **Many years later, facing the firing squad, Colonel Aureliano Buendia would remember that remote afternoon when his father took him to discover ice. Macondo was then a village of twenty houses of mud and canestalks constructed on the bank of a river of diaphanous waters which rushed through a bed of stones, polished, white and enormous like prehistoric eggs. (71;11)**

We are thus situated in the midst of a time that stretches endlessly backward, to the founding of the village and beyond, even to a time of "prehistoric eggs," and that stretches forward to sometime "many years later" when a very dramatic event will occur. Thus, from the very beginning, the author has prepared us to move constantly back and forth through time.

When the firing-squad scene does occur, several chapters later, it is something of an anticlimax. The colonel is not shot, after all: his brother saves him, and the firing squad happily switches sides and follows the colonel. But that's all right, because by that time García Márquez has hooked our interest with a number of other devices, including other flashforwards and, especially, our growing sympathy for the members of the Buendia clan. By this time, in other words, we keep reading because we care about these people.

Sometimes a coming event (or nonevent) is announced by a character, as when Amaranta declares that her foster sister Rebeca will never marry Pietro Crespi, and later when she prepares for her own impending death by weaving a shroud and Ursula announces she will die when it stops raining. And sometimes it is mentioned in the anonymous voice of the narrator, as when the destruction of Macondo is foretold at the beginning of the fifteenth chapter: "The events that would deliver the mortal blow to Macondo began to be apparent when the son of Meme Buendia was brought to the house." (365;272)

Repetition Of Events And Processes

Another important technique is repetition. Similar events keep occurring, generation after generation. The technique is not hidden, but rather is made very obvious to the reader. First, there is the literal repetition of names, especially the two men's names, Jose Arcadio and Aureliano, with minor variations from one generation to the next, but also of the women's names Ursula, Amaranta, and Remedios (the third of whom is known by the nickname, Meme). Certain character traits are supposed to go with the names. Thus, all the Jose Arcadios are supposedly exuberant and headstrong, all the Aurelianos contemplative and solitary - at least, this is Ursula Iguaran's theory, though in one generation (Jose Arcadio Segundo and his twin brother, Aureliano Segundo) the personalities seem to have been reversed.

There are also repetitions of processes; growth and decay, frenzied attempts to unlock the secrets of the universe (an obsession of the founder, Jose Arcadio Buendia, and of most of his male descendants down through the last Aureliano), desperate sexual passions (chiefly but not exclusively a male trait in the family), attempts at restoration and renewal of the house (mostly by the women, but also at one point by Aureliano Segundo, during the five years' rain). And there are repetitions of events, such as the long rains and attacks of forgetfulness (in the form of a plague in the early days of Macondo, as a result of government propaganda after the banana workers' massacre). To make sure these points are not missed, the characters, especially Ursula and, near the very end, Pilar Ternera, comment on the repetitions. At one point, Ursula has a brief conversation with her great-grandson Jose Arcadio Segundo and "realized she was giving the same reply she had received from Colonel Aureliano Buendia in his condemned-man's cell [many years and many pages earlier], and once more shuddered with the proof that time did not pass ... but kept spinning in circles." (409;310)

It is Pilar Ternera, now well over one-hundred forty-five years old, who perceives the real role of repetition in the Buendia family history and, not incidentally, in the structure of this novel: she had learned, the narrator says, " that the history of the family was a meshing of gears of unalterable repetitions, a turning wheel that would have kept spinning into eternity, if it had not been for the progressive and irremediable wearing down of the axle." (470;364)

Repetitions Break Down The System

This then is one way of visualizing the structure of the novel: not a circle, because the repetition of events does not bring us back to the place we started, but a spiral, in which every repetition "wears away the axle," until the whole system, including both the constant attempts to renew Macondo and the reproduction of the Buendia clan, breaks down.

Mystery Of The Narrator

Mention of Pilar's insight raises another important technical issue: the narrative voice. Who is this narrator? He or she knows the whole history of the Buendias better than any of them know it. But the narrator is not quite omniscient. For example, the opening sentence (quoted earlier) and Pilar's insight into the "axle" of time are two of the very few places where the narrator claims to be able to read a character's thoughts. Generally, we get to know characters from close observation of what they say and do, and we have to infer what they may be thinking. The narrator's knowledge also fails us in the one great unresolved mystery: Jose Arcadio, elder son of the founder, is murdered in his bed, but no one ever knows by whom. The narrator is also ignorant of who guns down all of the colonel's illegitimate sons and, in fact, seems as surprised as we are when the last survivor from among these sons appears in Macondo and is also shot down.

There are two likely candidates for narrator. One is Melquiades, the gypsy magician and wise man, who (we find out at the very end) had already written the whole history of Macondo before it happened. In that case, the novel *One Hundred Years of Solitude* that we are reading in Spanish (or English) is the very same as the manuscripts of Melquiades, written in Sanskrit.

There are two problems with this theory. First, the epigraph to the manuscripts, "The first of the line is tied to a tree and the last is being eaten by ants," is not the epigraph of the book we have been reading. Second, and more damaging to the theory, the narrator does not sound like Melquiades, but is much more naive and unsophisticated. The narrator who has been watching Melquiades, but does not think or speak like the old gypsy.

The other likely candidate is the town itself, a kind of collective voice of its people. García Márquez has used such a narrator before, in the short story, "Montiel's Widow," and perhaps that is what he is doing here. But if the town no longer exists, because it is destroyed at the end of the book, then how can it tell its own history?

This is a puzzle we do not need to resolve. The narrator's voice is that of a very observant, apparently objective reporter, much as García Márquez himself was for many years. Of course, the objectivity is more apparent than real: this narrator is clearly on the side of the workers against the banana company, and just as clearly for good wholesome sex and against sexual repression. But by maintaining the tone of objectivity, the reporter/narrator is able to describe the most bizarre events without comment, knowing only what he (or she) has seen and not claiming, at least until the very end, to know what it all means.

"Magic Realism" Or "The Marvelous Real"

It is this reporting of fantastic, bizarre events in a perfectly straight, seemingly objective tone that is what has been called "magic **realism**" or "the marvelous real," the technique, or attitude, most popularly identified with García Márquez's writings. The two terms are similar in meaning, but they have a little different history.

Magic **realism**, according to the *Oxford Companion to English Literature* (1985:606), is a term coined by the German writer Franz Roh in 1925, to describe works of art that are realistic in style but represent imaginary or fantastic scenes. More recently, it has been applied to the works of several writers of fiction, García Márquez prominent among them, as well as Gunter Grass (Germany), John Fowles (England), Italo Calvino (Italy), and several others. "Magic realist novels and stories have, typically, a strong narrative drive, in which the recognizably realistic mingles with the unexpected and the inexplicable, and in which elements of dream, fairy-story, or mythology combine with the everyday, often in a mosaic or kaleidoscopic pattern of refraction and recurrence." (*Oxford Companion*, 606–607)

"The marvelous real" is a translation of Cuban novelist Alejo Carpentier's phrase, lo real maravilloso. Carpentier was referring to a similar phenomenon - realistic portrayal of fantastic events - but with a peculiarly Latin American twist: for Carpentier, what seemed fantastic was, in Latin America, absolutely, literally real. In other words, there are in Latin America historical events and geological and other wonders that are so amazing they cannot be exaggerated - actually they must be told completely straight, objectively, to make them seem believable. This is an argument that García Márquez himself has made many times, notably in his Nobel Prize acceptance speech, and there is definitely something to it. The splendor and volume of the waters crashing down Iguazu Falls in Paraguay (a glimpse of which is seen in the movie, The Mission), for example, is beyond our capacity to exaggerate, as are the great obsessions of conquistadores, warriors, and rebels of the region, or the cruelties of its dictators.

Some of the magical events in *One Hundred Years of Solitude* are total inventions that serve to suggest the credulity of the townspeople (who may or may not be the same as the narrator). For example, old Father Nicanor Reyna, who levitates twelve centimeters above the ground after drinking hot chocolate. Others are exaggerations of quite plausible and familiar occurrences, or a literalizing of familiar myths.

For example, the founders' great-granddaughter Remedios the beautiful ascends to heaven one day when she goes out to hang up the sheets. We have already noted, in chapter II, that much as this is literally impossible, such a story was told about a girl in García Márquez's hometown. Another apparent exaggeration is that Colonel Aureliano Buendia has fathered seventeen sons by as many women during the war, and that all these young men come and stay in the Buendia house for a time. The author remembers that his maternal grandfather, Colonel Nicolas Márquez, did indeed have a great number of illegitimate children, possibly as many as seventeen, who were fathered during the war, and were always well-received when they visited the house.

Enumerating The Fantastic

One of García Márquez's favorite devices for making the fantastic sound realistic is his habit, perhaps picked up in years of newspaper reporting, of giving precise figures for things. Thus, the heavy rains that fall on Macondo - a perfectly normal, but impressive, event in northeastern Colombia - are said to last precisely four years, eleven months, and two days. To a child watching it rain, it might seem to last that long. Three thousand workers are massacred by troops during the banana strike. Colonel Aureliano Buendia fights, and loses, precisely thirty-two wars, and so on.

When we read of such amazing events told in such an objective and naive voice, we realize it is up to us, the readers, to interpret their meaning. Whoever is narrating is simply too literal-minded and simple to have trustworthy opinions.

Irony At Several Levels

The realistic description of impossible events is also an example, at the level of language, of García Márquez's **irony**. Irony is the use of words, images, and so on, to convey the opposite of their intended meaning. García Márquez employs **irony** on several levels. Sometimes a single word, such as a character's name, suggests something opposite to the character's personality: for example, Prudencio Aguilar, who is not the least bit "prudent" (see chapter V of this Note).

Sometimes a character's style of speech is ironic. For example, in the chapter on the banana workers' strike, the court uses very stiff, pompous language to state something that is ridiculous: that the banana workers do not exist, because they are technically not "employees" of the firm - an evasion of the government's responsibility that has tragic consequences. Another example is Fernanda's long-winded proclamations of her religious devotion. These are obviously expressions, not of Christian love, but of extreme self-centeredness and rigidity. The apparently patriotic declarations of Liberals and Conservatives alike also have nothing to do with loyalty to the country, but are really about the narrow ambitions of the politicians.

More subtly, what the narrator or the characters say may sometimes contradict what the reader knows to be true. There are many examples in the solemn announcements of Jose Arcadio Buendia, including his finding that ice "is the great invention of our time." Much later, the apparent progress brought by the banana company to Macondo turns out not to be a progress at all, but a prelude to devastation.

Still more subtly, García Márquez has reserved a final ironic twist for us: in the last chapter, he suggests that the whole book is not what it appears to be, but may be, like the town and the family, a creation of the gypsy Melquiades, or perhaps (when he has a character say "Literature is the greatest toy for fooling people") simply a hallucination.

The effect of **irony** is generally comic, but as we can see from these few examples, García Márquez also frequently uses it to underscore a tragedy. Even the novel's last sentence, which appears to be giving the moral of the story, is ironic. Why should "the bloodlines condemned to one hundred years of solitude" not have "a second opportunity on earth"? and how does any family get such a terrible condemnation? The real lessons of this book, if we are bent on finding moral lessons, have to do with the nature of power, of love, of solitude, but also of capitalist development and of literature itself.

The Advantage Of The Unreliable Narrator

In the end, whatever sense the novel makes is up to the reader to figure out. Fortunately, we are provided with so many clues to the novel's themes that we should have no trouble coming to our own conclusions. Thus, this pseudo-objective, reportorial narrative voice serves the author well: it enables him to present all the relevant information while inviting us to make the obvious, and the less obvious, connections. We the readers then can have the extremely satisfying feeling we have "got" it. And if we read it a second time, we get it at another level, because we see more connections - and rereading it, we, in effect, give the Buendias their "second opportunity on earth."

In this way, García Márquez has played his biggest trick, not so much on us his readers as on the novel as a literary **genre**. He has taken us into his confidence, so that both he and we at the end see just how the novel was constructed - not how he struggled to write it, but how he finally designed it to make it work as a whole.

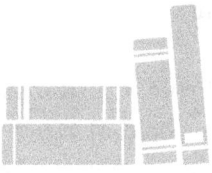

CHAPTER-BY-CHAPTER

TEXTUAL ANALYSIS

CHAPTERS 1-3

This analysis will focus on themes, techniques, and symbolism in each chapter, to show how each part contributes to the whole. Since this will be an analysis, no attempt will be made to summarize. Students who desire chapter-by-chapter plot summaries and who read Spanish may refer to the Spanish-language commentaries listed in the "Selected Bibliography," especially the one published by Vosgos, where summaries and discussions of each chapter run for several pages. However, even if language is not a problem, trying to reconstruct the story from such summaries will probably be more difficult, and certainly less fun, than reading the novel itself. The most rewarding approach will be for the student first to read the chapter in the novel, and then to read the following analyses for a fuller understanding of that chapter.

The novel is divided into twenty untitled and unnumbered sections, here treated as chapters. Following all quotations, the page numbers from the Joset edition of *Cien anaos de soledad* are followed by those from the Rabassa translation. Four of the chapters will be discussed at more length than the others: the first two wherein García Márquez first displays most of the techniques that will be used throughout the book, and the last two because their complex symbolism suggests alternative readings of the book.

CHAPTER 1 (INTRODUCTION TO THE WORLD OF MACONDO)

Rules Of This Fictional Universe

Like a game, *One Hundred Years of Solitude* has rules that the reader needs to understand in order to grasp a fuller meaning. García Márquez establishes the most fundamental of these rules immediately, in the very first lines.

The first rule is that time flows forward and backward freely, so that any given moment is to be understood as part of a continuous flow of time. This is established in the opening sentence:

> Many years later, facing the firing squad, Colonel Aureliano Buendía would remember that remote afternoon when his father took him to discover ice. (71; 11)

The opening phrase, "Many years later," before we even know "Later than what?" signals the importance of later events for understanding the present. In this novel, unlike our normal experience, the present is influenced by the future as much as by the past, because some things must happen now (present) to fulfill a prophecy (future) that was made in the past.

The second rule is that the reader must expect abrupt changes of pace. The phrase "facing a firing squad" suddenly confronts us with violence, whereas the next long clause takes us to a peaceful "remote afternoon," and so on. There will be many such abrupt shifts of tone and pace, giving a sense of instability or fragility to even the most peaceful, idyllic episodes.

A third rule is that ordinary things are made extraordinary, and *vice versa.* Could ice be so wonderful that its memory would fill the mind of a man facing a firing squad? Here, it can be.

The extraordinariness of seemingly ordinary things is also conveyed by the author's painstakingly detailed description of inanimate objects, especially peculiar objects. This is apparent realism used to establish its opposite, a magical quality that is beyond realism, in other words, surrealism. The extraordinariness of the ordinary is made explicit by Melquíades when he says, "Things have their own life, it's just a matter of arousing their soul" (72;11).

An example of a "thing" with its "own life" is the suit of armor that José Arcadio Buendia finds with the magnets; it is described in such detail it seems still to be inhabited by its fifteenth-century owner. And, happily for the author's purpose, that discovery also reminds us of the continuous flow of time, because it brings the fifteenth century into the nineteenth-century "present" of this first chapter. This trick is repeated with the discovery of the galleon (83;20).

Conversely, seemingly extraordinary events are treated as perfectly ordinary. In this chapter, we have the amazing travels of Melquiades to and from Macondo, while the *Macondinos* (inhabitants of Macondo) themselves cannot find a route to the outside world. There are also the marvelous devices of the "new Gypsies," such as "the multipurpose machine that could be used both to sew buttons and to reduce fever," and so on (89;24), quite extraordinary things that seem unimportant to the narrator. Later, there will be returns from the dead, flying carpets, a levitating priest, and other wonders, all told as though they were perfectly normal.

A fourth rule is that everything is bigger than life. Exaggeration, sometimes comic and sometimes tragic, establishes the scale of the novel—that is, outsized. Examples include the tremendous power of Melquiades's magnets, José Arcadio Buendía's scientific fanaticism, and the extreme naivete of the people of Macondo.

THEMES

The founding of Macondo not only begins the novel but also suggests three other great beginnings. The first is the beginning of the world as recounted in Genesis, evoked in the sentence "The world was so new, many things did not have names, and to mention them one had to point with a finger." The founders of Macondo, like Adam, will have to give them names.

Second, the founding reflects the history of Spanish settlement throughout the Americas, which almost everywhere started with "a village of twenty houses of mud and canestalks built on the bank of a river." To sixteenth-century mapmakers, explorers, and storytellers, the genesis of the world and the discovery of the New World were closely associated; America was thought to be either literally the Garden of Eden, miraculously rediscovered, or someplace very much like it. And it was true that many things—animals, plants, rivers, mountains, and of course the people they called "Indians"—were so new to the Europeans that, like Adam, they did not have names for them.

But there is also a third kind of beginning in this chapter: the beginnings of scientific consciousness. An outside agent, the gypsy Melquíades, alerts José Arcadio Buendía to the existence of a marvelous reality outside of his experience, and encourages him to speculate and experiment. Although Melquíades is essentially benevolent, unlike the serpent who tempts Eve in the Garden of Eden, the knowledge he brings is a mixed blessing. It leads the founder, Buendia, to absurd and destructive experiments, such as nearly burning down the house with a magnifying glass and converting his wife's stock of gold doubloons into a worthless lump of alloy stuck to a pot. But it also leads him to the discovery that the "earth is round, like an orange," The irony here is that the narrator treats this assertion as being just as wild as the experiments, and seems to sympathize with the founder's wife, Ursula Iguarán, who thinks her husband has gone quite mad.

This scene is critical for defining the contrasting characters of the husband and wife: he, a wildly impractical and fanatical pursuer of ultimate truths; she, a sensible and hardworking matriarch devoted to nothing grander than the preservation and education of her family. Only a few pages later, power passes definitively from him to her when she refuses to let him take the family off into the wilderness.

References

The chapter is peppered with historical and literary allusions, including the following:

The Jews of Amsterdam (72;12): An important intellectual community that thrived more than one hundred years before the probable date of Melquíades's visit to Macondo, so the gypsy is a bit out of date. One of their most illustrious members was the lensmaker and philosopher Baruch Spinoza (1632–1677).

The Monk Hermann (74;13): The German Benedictine Hermann von Richenau, called Hermann the Lame (b. 1013), author of works on astrology.

Nostradamus (76;15): French astrologer and physician (1503–1566), author of the famous encoded prophecies, *Centuries astrologiques* (1555).

Philosopher's egg (77;17): The alchemists' symbol of totality.

Formulas of Moses and Zosimus (78;16): A reference to the two great branches of religious/mystical knowledge, the Jewish and the Greek; Zosimus was a Greek alchemist of the third century A.D.

Great Teaching (78;16): Also called *Opus alchimicum*, the operations relating to the transformation of matter until the alchemist achieves the Philosopher's Stone, representing spiritual perfection.

Nasciancenos (79;17): Nacianzo, in Cappadocia (ancient region of Asia Minor, west of Armenia), was the home of St. Gregory of Nacianzo (330P–390), father of the Greek church and bishop of Constantinople.

Sir Francis Drake (81;19): English corsair (1540–1596) who did actually attack Riohacha, a port on the north coast of Colombia.

CHAPTER 2
(INCEST AND LOSS OF INNOCENCE)

Time And Repetition

The flashback to pirate raids of the sixteenth century reminds the reader of the continuous flow of time. Another device serving the same purpose is repetition, especially the repetition of names and events in the family. The device is extended into the past: we learn that there were a José Arcadio and an Aureliano Buendia as far back as the sixteenth century.

Incest, Sex, And Monsters

Ursula Iguaran's obsessive fear of incest is really a fear of engendering monsters, whether iguanas (a play on her own last name) or a child with a pig's tail. The tail that was already appeared in a relative is described as like a corkscrew, or spiral, with a tuft of hair on the end. Although this will not be apparent until much later, the shape of the tail mimics the shape of the novel; the birth of a human with a pig's tail (Chapter 20) will mark the spiraling of the book to its conclusion. Incest is suggested again when José Arcadio, junior, makes love for the first time and imagines the face of his mother, Ursula. (100;34)

The Buendia men are very violent love-makers: José Arcadio, senior, trembling with fury, drives a lance into the ground to emphasize his demand for sex with Ursula (95;29); his son and namesake possesses a huge phallus with which he nearly tears a young gypsy girl apart (106-107;39-40). The references to young José Arcadio's phallus are somewhat more explicit in the Spanish original, where it is dear that "the evidence" that the young gypsy "could not believe" was the pressure of his penis against her back. She turned and *"lo miro,"* that is, either saw "him" or saw "it," "with a tremulous smile." (106;39)

What the older gypsy woman says when she sees "his magnificent animal in repose" is, literally, "May God protect it for you." (107;40)

The Original Sin Of Macondo

In the book of Genesis, the first city (Enoch) is built by Cain after he has slain his brother Abel. The founding of Macondo is also precipitated by a murder, José Arcadio Buendia's killing of Prudencio Aguilar. Buendia sets off into the wilderness to escape Prudencio Aguilar's ghost, which introduces the theme of the continuing suffering of the dead and their visitations to the living.

Transparencies And Reflections

Mirrors and mirages *(expejos* and *espejismos)* will be recurrent images, along with lenses (e.g., the telescope and magnifying glass in the first chapter), the crystalline waters of the river and of the ice (in both the first and second chapters). José Arcadio Buendia's dream-image of the future town is "a noisy city with houses of walls of mirrors." (97;32) Reflection again suggests repetition, and transparency suggests insubstantiality. García Márquez cannot resist giving this image a comic turn, and has Buendia interpret his dream as meaning that in the future houses in the tropics will be built of ice.

Loss Of Innocence

Probably the most important theme in this chapter, along with incest, is the loss of innocence. The first is the seduction of José Arcadio, junior, by Pilar Ternera, followed by the young man's running away from home and the responsibilities of fatherhood. As a consequence of his actions, the whole town loses its Arcadian innocence: Ursula goes out looking for him and, five months later, returns to Macondo with a group of settlers. The newcomers will transform Macondo totally.

Notice that the new gypsies who visit Macondo are also not as innocent and well-meaning as the earlier group led by Melquíades; they are hustlers and tricksters rather than the bearers of important scientific truths. Here is also another example of García Márquez's irony, the inversion of the "ordinary" and the "extraordinary:" a flying carpet is treated as unremarkable, not even worth the attention of José Arcadio Buendía (the elder), who is devoted to his own mystical notion of progress.

CHAPTER 3
(MEMORY, AMNESIA, AND HISTORY)

In this chapter, Macondo leaves its prehistoric, Edenic, or Arcadian state (see comment on the name José Arcadio in Chapter 5) and begins to replicate the early stages of urban civilization: that is, it enters histone. Rather than describe this whole process, García Márquez gives a few very specific, carefully chosen details, from which we can infer the rest, such as: "shops and crafts workshops, and a permanent commercial route by which came the first Arabs with their slippers and necklaces." (113;44—here, as in a few other places, Rabassa's translation is less literal than literary.) Another detail indicating the transformation is that musical clocks (machine technology) replace the caged birds (nature), which are set free (114;45). Nevertheless, the town is still patriarchal and egalitarian: the founder oversees the disposition of land to the newcomers, so that no one is more favored than any other.

The arrival of eleven-year-old Rebeca reintroduces the theme of the unreliability of memory. She brings with her unmistakable evidence of a past—a bag containing her parents' bones—but it is a past that is indecipherable, since the girl herself will not speak of it nor can the Buendias remember knowing anybody by the names given in her letter of presentation.

Incidentally, these bones make a more bonelike noise in the original Spanish than in the English translation: "*cloqueante cacareo de galïina clueca*," an example of alliterative onomatopoeia (use of words to sound like the thing described). The literal translation, the "clucking of a broody hen" (117;48), misses the effect, since a "hen" is in this image only to introduce the raucous sound *clueca* ("brooding").

Does God Exist?

The "plague" of insomnia leads to amnesia, described as an "idiocy without a past." (120;50) Ignorance of the past is idiocy, García Márquez seems to be telling us, because it makes it impossible for us to act intelligently in the present. (This theme will be recurrent, most forcefully expressed in the final chapter.) The methods for combating the erosion of memory range from the fantastic—José Arcadio Buendía's imaginary memory machine—to the more practical writing down of names of objects, an evident metaphor for the inventories that have been the beginning of written history everywhere, from Sumer and ancient Egypt to the Mayan temple carvings. There is humor in the incongruity of information that José Arcadio Buendía considers important enough to record: the uses of a cow, along with the proposition "God exists." This, by the way, is a proposition that Buendía is already beginning to doubt and (in the next chapter) will abandon altogether; thus writing transmits both truths and more doubtful assertions.

The funniest comment on misreadings of the past is, of course, Pilar Ternera's attempt to invent history the same way she has been trying to read the future, by reading her tarot cards, and coming up with preposterous shadowy fables. Another ironic joke, is the inversion of what, in medieval Europe, was normal plague behavior: in Macondo it is the uninfected people who are required to carry a warning bell and are given a special label, the *durmientes* ("sleepers").

AN INCIDENT THAT BECOMES A MOVIE

Aureliano's encounter with the adolescent mulatto girl, prostituted by her grandmother (127–129;57–58), is here used to show his sexual excitement and innocence. The incident was later expanded by García Márquez into the short story and screenplay, "The Incredible and Sad Tale of Innocent Erendira and Her Heartless Grandmother," which was made into a successful film. (We shall come across other examples where García Márquez has woven together scenes from *One Hundred Years of Solitude* with his other works.)

After the amnesia episode, there remains one more important detail to insert Macondo fully into history: the town must become part of a larger political system. This is represented by the arrival of Apolinar Moscote, magistrate (*corregidor*) and the first representative of the central government to appear in Macondo.

There is a pun in José Arcadio Buendia's confrontation with Moscote that is only partly captured in the translation. *Corregidor* (which Rabassa translates as "judge") is an antiquated Spanish term for a justice of the peace, but it can also mean "corrector." It is in this sense that the naive Buendia understands the word when he tells Moscote, "We don't need a corrector here, because there is nothing to correct!" (133;61)

That Moscote is permitted to remain in town out of respect for his wife and daughters reveals an important and appealing aspect of Buendia's personality: his respect for family values above personal enmities.

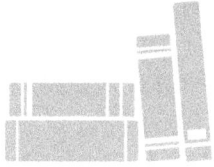

ONE HUNDRED YEARS OF SOLITUDE

TEXTUAL ANALYSIS

CHAPTERS 4-12

CHAPTER 4: THE PIONEERS FADE AWAY

The new stage in the town's history is symbolized by Ursula's reconstruction and enlargement of the house and her gala ball. Her "severe" guest list is "in reality a class selection," not, as the translation has it, merely "a high-class" list, but one drawn up according to class (137;65), including the original pioneers and their children and grandchildren, "except the family of Pilar Ternera" (emphasis added.) Pilar has become disreputable because of her illegitimate children. The **irony** here is that one of those bastards is Arcadio, Ursula's own grandson.

The ball is so exclusive that even the corregidor Apolinar Moscote and his family are snubbed. This grand social affair, with its comic mishaps - the jumbled music resulting from Jose Arcadio Buendia's tinkering with the pianola - is in effect the farewell party to the rustic manners of the pioneer families. Pietro Crespi, the Italian pianola man and dance master with fine table manners and "tight, flexible trousers," is a harbinger of a new, more sophisticated order.

Appropriately, the second, definitive death of Melquíades, the bearer of ancient mystical traditions, comes in this period when music is made by a pianola and real birds are feed from their cages to be replaced by mechanical singing clocks; the new Macondo has no need of or interest in his kind of (premechanical) wisdom. The founder himself, old Jose Arcadio Buendia, finally cannot cope with all the changes and goes completely mad, mentally stopping time in a perpetual Monday.

CHAPTER 5: AURELIANO'S REVOLT

A further sign of the times is the presence of Father Nicanor Reyna, who has come to the Macondo to marry Aureliano and Remedios and decides to stay. He intends to rescue the Macondinos from their scandalous customs, including living "according to natural law, without baptizing their children nor honoring the holy days" (158;85) - a fair summary of the frontier morality of the simpler, less complicated society that is now ending. To astound the Macondinos and win converts, the priest uses a rather pathetic magic trick - levitating a mere twelve centimeters, and only that with the help of hot chocolate. This contrasts with the behavior of Melquiades, who had presented far more impressive and useful marvels with no other aim than to enlighten.

The return of Jose Arcadio, junior, as a tattooed giant of enormous strength, and virility so astounding that the whores pay to have sex with him - another inversion of normal events - is an example of García Márquez's comic **irony**. Jose Arcadio's seduction of Rebeca again raises the **theme** of incest, whether actual or imagined (since, at the time, he and she think they are siblings).

From their new house, Jose Arcadio now deploys his vigor in hunting and in seizing his neighbor's lands. He is a kind of Paul Bunyan of the landed bourgeoisie, a man big enough to represent a whole class of exploiters that did, historically, emerge in this area after independence. Such expropriation was one of the underlying causes of the numerous civil wars.

His younger brother Aureliano will come to represent the other side in this conflict, the reform movement led by the anticlerical, democratic, petty bourgeoisie of the towns. When he revolts against the injustices of the Conservatives occupying Macondo, he also reveals two traits that he shares with his father: indignation and leadership. Aureliano's leadership of the rising of his twenty-one young companions is a parallel, in changed circumstances, to Jose Arcadio Buendia's leadership of these young men's fathers (also numbering twenty-one) when he founded Macondo.

CHAPTER 6: WAR COMES TO MACONDO

The young Arcadio, left in command of Macondo by his uncle Aureliano, becomes "the cruelest governor Macondo had ever had," the first of the Buendias to be morally corrupted by power. When Arcadio is about to execute Apolinar Moscote, Ursula (Arcadio's grandmother) storms out of the house and spanks him in front of his men, in a funny and touching reassertion of matriarchal values. But this is a short-lived victory of humanity over the cruelties of war.

Idealism And Self-Interest

One of Arcadio's official acts is to create a land registry that legitimizes the titles of his father, Jose Arcadio, to lands he has usurped, suggesting the self-interest that gets mixed in with the idealistic causes of the civil war. This one case also stands for the consolidation of the power of the landed gentry generally, which was occurring in the early nineteenth century in most of Latin America. (There are Buendias on both sides of the conflict over land, as we shall see when Aureliano institutes land reform.)

Arcadio's rapid evolution into a tyrant and his recklessly heroic and futile last battle anticipate, in miniature, what will be the much larger but equally futile saga of Colonel Aureliano Buendia.

Amaranta meanwhile has been encouraging the attentions of Pietro Crespi, teasing him, and when she spurns him, he is so distraught he goes home and cuts his wrists. Her self-immolation, in reaction to his suicide, is perhaps a strange, inward-directed expression of grief, sealing her fate as an extremely solitary, uncommunicative person.

As we have already seen, an insistent **theme** of the novel is the imaginative power of writing and the difficulties of reading, that is, deciphering, a text. Accordingly, one of the last images in this chapter is Arcadio, just before pissing in his pants because he is about to be shot, remembering "letter by letter the encyclicals chanted by Melquiades" (198;119). He remembers them, but of course he has not understood them; that will be for a much later generation.

CHAPTER 7: THE COLONEL'S PRIDE; DEATH OF THE FOUNDER

When Ursula visits Aureliano in his cell, he says he has "had the impression that I had already gone through all this." (201;122) In reality it is not Aureliano, but the reader who has "already gone through all this" many times, because we have had premonitions of Aureliano's impending execution since the first sentence of the first chapter, with several later references. The reader has also just "gone through" a kind of rehearsal, the execution of Arcadio in the preceding chapter.

When Aureliano expresses his surprise at changes in the town, his mother asks, "What did you expect? Time passes." He replies, "Yes, but not that much." (201;123) This dialogue makes explicit the **theme** of the repetition of events, making time seem to pass "not that much." There is a deliberate confusion of the reader's sense of when things "really" occur, achieved in part by the technique of describing an event in finer detail as a flashforward or flashback than at the moment of occurrence. For example, we now learn for the first time what Aureliano was wearing when his father took him to discover ice, an event that occurred in the first chapter. This technique, used repeatedly in the novel, makes the present seem less "real" than an imagined future or a remembered past.

In any case, the much-predicted execution of Aureliano does not take place: Jose Arcadio saves him, responding not to ideology or a moral imperative but to the elemental bond of kinship. The incident also highlights Aureliano's enormous power over other men, since the Conservative firing squad is only too happy to switch sides and follow him into the Liberal army.

A Parody Of Cortazar?

Jose Arcadio is later murdered in his home, no one knows by whom, and the blood from the wound winds its way through the town into the kitchen to where his mother, Ursula, is working, again affirming that for him, even in death, kinship is the strongest bond. (The image of the unstoppable line of blood, incidentally, may be an intentional **parody** of a short story by García Márquez's friend and colleague Julio Cortazar; one is never quite sure just how seriously to take García Márquez. Refer to "The Lines of the Hand," in Cortazar's Cronopios and Famas, originally published in 1962.) "This was perhaps the only mystery that was never solved in Macondo" (208;129). Rebeca thereupon shuts herself up in their house, becoming another of the extreme solitaries in the family of solitary individuals, to be "forgotten" by the town, victim of another case of amnesia.

Colonel Aureliano Buendia appears to be immortal and ubiquitous, returning triumphant, surviving numerous assassination attempts, and continuing to hold the loyalty of his friends. In effect he is immortal and ubiquitous, because he symbolizes not one but dozens of rebel chieftains, or caudillos, in nineteenth-century Latin America.

When his comrade-in-arms and oldest friend, Colonel Gerineldo Márquez, proposes marriage to Amaranta, she rejects him with these words: "you love Aureliano so much you want to marry me because you can't marry him." (215;135) In fact, men like Colonel Aureliano Buendia did command great loyalty and affection from their subordinates. García Márquez makes it clear that the caudillo does not reciprocate: Aureliano's first reaction to an earlier telegram threatening the execution of Gerineldo was "Great! Now we've got a telegraph in Macondo!" (207;128)

In keeping with the **theme** of writing and deciphering, Aureliano comes to understand his own thoughts by writing out his experiences in verse. In this way, he comes to the terrible realization that, as he tells Gerineldo, that "I'm fighting for pride." As for what his friend calls "the great Liberal party," Aureliano declares that it "doesn't mean anything to anybody." (213;133) There has been a substantial erosion of the Colonel's idealism and values from his earlier days, when he thought it important to redistribute lands and protect civilian lives.

Understanding The Colonel's Pride

It is important to understand the Colonel's pride (orgullo in Spanish). It is not, as a North American might think, the kind of satisfaction one takes in one's possessions or accomplishments. The Colonel is not proud of anything he has done or owns, in fact is not even interested in these things; he is as quick to destroy as to create, and is unconcerned about whether or not he is dressed in rags. Rather, his is a pride that has been critically important in Latin American history, a kind that is associated with notions of masculine honor. The Colonel's pride is a refusal to submit to any power but his own. The Mexican revolutionary leader Pancho Villa had this kind of pride, and so do many contemporary political leaders in Latin America; it makes for colorful rebels and impossible subordinates, and complicates political or business negotiations tremendously - since neither party can back down. In the Colonel's case, it extends to refusing to modify one's plans to take into consideration the needs of anyone else. Pride, then, is another word for solitude.

The death of old Jose Arcadio Buendia, predicted long distance by Aureliano, brings the return of the Indian Cataure "for the burial of the king." The presence of Cataure, plus the visits of (the ghost of) Prudencio Aguilar to Buendia just before his death, take us back to the days of the founding of Macondo. These reminders function like the strains of an opening melody repeated at the end of a symphonic movement; they mark a closing, in this case of the narrative cycle of the founding of Macondo. To further mark the occasion, a mysterious "drizzle of minuscule yellow flowers" accompanies the founder's death. If the existence of God has been doubtful in Macondo, there is no doubt that supernatural spirits of some kind watch over the town's leading family.

CHAPTER 8: THE COLONEL CORRUPTED

The chapter has two main themes: the unconsummated incest between Amaranta and her nephew Aureliano Jose, and the corruption of Colonel Aureliano Buendia by pride and power.

The Colonel's stupendous plan for "the unification of the Federalist forces of Central America, to sweep away conservative regimes from Alaska to Patagonia," (222;141) is an example of the marvelous real, that is, of something that seems fantastic but actually has a realistic basis: it is on the scale of a real plan promoted by Simon Bolivar (1783–1830) to unify the newly independent American republics. The Colonel's travels abroad and his attempts to mount invasions from exile also recapitulate the experience of dozens of real Latin American revolutionaries, from Bolivar to Fidel Castro. The peace accord, in which the Liberal political elite agrees to sell out its principles in exchange for a few ministerial posts, has also been a familiar kind of event. Colonel Aureliano Buendia's reaction to this sellout is to attempt seven uprisings in the first year of the agreement, which shows how far pride can drive a man. (See the comment on "pride" in the analysis of chapter 7, page 69.)

That the Colonel has had sex with countless women, without ever learning their names or seeing their faces, and that he has in this way fathered seventeen sons he neither knows nor cares about, are further signs of his emotional solitude. These sons also all have a "solitary" look - so the condition is hereditary. Their simultaneous arrival in Macondo, independently, is one more marvelous event.

Degrading Ideals

The Colonel's other son, Aureliano Jose, has meanwhile "learned" from another soldier that the purpose of "this war against the priests" is "so one can marry his own mother" (225;145) or, what is of greater interest to Aureliano Jose, his aunt. This interpretation of Liberal doctrine is a sign of how far the ideals of the movement have become degraded in the long years of warfare, and also represents a further weakening of the taboo against incest. When Amaranta reminds him of the danger of offspring "with pigs' tails," he answers in almost the same words his grandfather, Jose Arcadio Buendia, used with Ursula: it wouldn't matter, he says, "Even if you were to bear armadillos." (226;145). His grandfather, in the second chapter, had said "iguanas." Events are repeated, but never in precisely the same way.

The death of Aureliano Jose illustrates again the fierce Buendia pride: he is shot by the captain of the garrison because he refuses to be frisked. That the captain is almost immediately gunned down by anonymous towns-people shows the strength of the loyalty of the Macondinos to the Colonel and his family.

Humanity Versus Pride

The extent of the corruption of the Colonel's humanity by his pride is shown when he orders the execution of Jose Raquel Moncada, his compadre (co-godfather), who also happens to be an enemy general. The friendship between the two nominal enemies is modeled on that between the real Liberal general, Rafael Uribe Uribe, and the Conservative general, Pedro Nel Ospina, who in the midst of the war in 1990 had exchanged friendly letters advocating "civilizing" the conflict. Although the text does not make this explicit, it is likely that the two men are literally co-godfathers, that is, that General Moncada has baptized one or more of the seventeen sons of the Colonel who arrive while Moncada is governing the town. In any case, the use of the term indicates a very close and sacred tie. (Moncada also calls Ursula comadre, the female equivalent, and she calls him compadre.)

The Colonel tries to explain his action to Moncada with the sophism, "Remember, compadre, it is not I who shoots you. You are going to be shot by the revolution." Moncada replies with elegant simplicity: "Vete a la mierda, compadre" - literally, "Go to the shit, compadre" (235;153), rather stronger than the English "go to Hell." By coupling the strongest possible expletive with the strongest possible term of masculine bonding, García Márquez has packed a heavy charge of **irony** into this five-word retort. By giving the Conservative general the best line, the author signals that his sympathies are clearly with Moncada.

CHAPTER 9: THE COLONEL ENDS HIS WARS

Like his father before him, the Colonel begins to lose contact with the world, as his telegraph messages show. He reaches the extreme of self-isolation when he orders a chalk circle drawn around him and refuses to let anyone, even his mother, come closer than two meters (not "ten feet," as the translation says, which would be more than three meters). (241;159)

The widow of General Moncada turns him away with a phrase that sums up women's social position throughout the novel and in much of Latin America, even today: "Don't enter, Colonel. You may rule in your war, but I rule in my house." (241;159) This is the only occasion in the novel where a man refuses to accept a woman's "home rule": the Colonel orders her house sacked and burned. This is clear evidence that he is no longer bound by even the strongest, most traditional of scruples. "You're rotting alive," Gerineldo warns him. (241;159)

The underhanded murder of a rival Liberal general, Teofilo Vargas, suggests that the rot has even affected his pride. The rules of manly honor would require that he face Vargas, man to man. How readily power corrupts a leader is stated in so many words by the narrator, not only with respect to Aureliano Buendia but regarding all such chieftains: "His orders were carried out before they were given, even before he had conceived them, and always went much further than he would have dared to take them." (242;160)

Futile Years Of War

The Liberal party comprises lawyers portrayed as being like vultures, but they have no difficulty persuading the Colonel to give up everything he's gained for the Liberal cause: land reform, anticlericalism, and the "aspiration for equality of rights between natural and legitimate children." (244;162) These drastic concessions show that the years of warfare have been utterly futile. The turning point comes after he orders the execution of his oldest comrade, Gerineldo Márquez, and then spends the night trying to break "the hard shell of his solitude," i.e., to recover some compassion for others. What results, though, is not love but a new burst of pride. He decides to end the wars by force rather than negotiation. The two years he spends fighting to end the war - one year to get the government to offer acceptable conditions, another to impose his authority on other Liberal commanders so as to accept the conditions - reflect what the real General Uribe Uribe did at the turn of the century.

Consistency Of The Imagination

At the capitulation to the Conservatives, a young rebel colonel arrives with a treasure of seventy-two gold bricks. This scene had been anticipated in García Márquez's earlier novella, *No One Writes to the Colonel*, so by mentioning it here the author connects the two books. García Márquez's imaginary world is amazingly consistent.

Colonel Aureliano Buendia's suicide is intended to be his final prideful act; its failure condemns him to serve a long and bitter penance for his lovelessness.

The end of the Colonel's wars is celebrated by another renewal of the old house by Ursula, which, as always, signals the inauguration of a new narrative cycle.

CHAPTER 10: GAMES OF THE TWINS

The twins, Jose Arcadio Segundo and Aureliano Segundo, so similar in appearance that they switch identities at will, are composites of the traits of the earlier bearers of those names.

Ursula, now over one hundred years old and blind, suspects the boys have become permanently switched, because Jose Arcadio Segundo behaves more like the Aurelianos of the family (pensive, withdrawn) and Aureliano Segundo more like the Jose Arcadios (impulsive and outgoing), but in fact both twins are complex, alternating from outgoing to withdrawn, active to passive, at different moments in their lives. This is presumably why García Márquez creates ambiguity as to which is which.

As a boy, Aureliano Segundo spends hours poring over Melquiades's manuscripts, but without success. In this connection, the spirit of Melquiades says a quite remarkable thing to him, which appears to have got slightly garbled in translation. That the statement is of a special kind is clear because García Márquez (in the Spanish text) sets it off in quotation marks, a punctuation he rarely uses. (Dialogue is generally indicated by a dash before statements.) Speaking of the manuscripts, Melquiades's words are: "Nadie debe conocer su sentido mientras no hayan cumplido cien anos." (Joset, 262) Rabassa gives us: "No one must know their meaning until he has reached one hundred years of age." (177) The sentence actually means, "No one must know their meaning until one hundred years have passed," but as Janes points out:

> **The Spanish sentence also contains a pun that the translation necessarily obscures: "No one must know their meaning when they haven't finished [reading] One Hundred Years [of Solitude]." ... The phrase one hundred years appears only two other times in the novel, both referring to the manuscripts at the end, and one in another pun. (Janes, 1981:59)**

The "other pun' is the final sentence of the book, which we shall get to in due course. Here García Márquez appears to be giving readers a clue, or perhaps just a tease, as to the auto-subversion that the book will undergo just as it is ending.

Jose Arcadio Segundo, meanwhile, raises fighting cocks, which was the old passion of his great-grandfather that led to the murder of Prudencio Aguilar and the founding of Macondo; the founder's prohibition against cockfighting in Macondo is not forgotten (Ursula remembers), but ignored by the younger generation. Jose Arcadio Segundo also assists the priest, and when the Colonel's old Liberal and anticlerical comrade Gerineldo Márquez reproaches him, he answers, "It seems to me I turned out Conservative" - as though it were a destiny, not a decision (263;177). Actually, he will be the brother who later carries on the Colonel's tradition of social rebellion.

Folklore Theme

When Aureliano Segundo lies with his brother's womanfriend, Petra Cotes, she is unaware of the substitution - not very credible in the real world, but a familiar **theme** in folklore (cf. the biblical Jacob's substituting for his twin Esau in receiving their father's birthright).

Petra Cotes is a kind of fertility goddess, who is infertile herself (she has no children), but causes great fertility in Aureliano Segundo's animals and crops; he is convinced that their energetic lovemaking produces this magical displacement of sexual fertility, which makes him one of the richest men in Macondo. His riotous parties are much like those that reportedly took place in García Márquez's hometown in the early 1900s.

A complex anecdote recalls the extravagant enterprises of Jose Arcadio Buendia, the founder, and shows how the same impulse in his great-grandson produces something ridiculous and ribald rather than heroic. Jose Arcadio Segundo, financed by his brother, dredges the river to make it navigable - with the same energy and dedication with which his ancestor strove to hack a trail to the outside world. Despite the scoffing of his neighbors, he at last brings to Macondo the "first and only boat that ever moored in the town." (272;185-186) The boat is really no more than a log raft, whose passengers are French matrons (brothel madams) whose cultural contribution to the town will be new arts of lovemaking.

The sister of the twins, the beautiful and simple-minded Remedios, illustrates one of García Márquez's recurrent themes: the only way to be completely pure and innocent is to be too dumb to perceive evil. Fernanda, the girl from the Andes, is the counterexample: she is also beautiful, but selfish and on guard against evil even where there is none.

The Colonel's activity in his workshop, making little goldfishes that he exchanges for gold coins, which he melts down to make more fishes, recapitulates his military career: doing in order to undo.

CHAPTER 11: RETURN OF THE SEVENTEEN AURELIANOS

The remote, grim town in the mountains where Aureliano Segundo finds Fernanda is a caricature of the kind of place where García Márquez spent his unhappy high school years, and Fernanda herself is a cruel caricature of the people there. Despite her youth and beauty, she is a severe, humorless woman who is not much fun for her new husband; Aureliano Segundo soon returns to sleep with his concubine, Petra Cotes. When Fernanda finds out, she imposes a single condition: that he be sure not to die in his concubine's bed, since that would expose the relationship to the public. Fernanda is the character more interested in appearances than in substance.

Brought up to believe in her own superiority, Fernanda claims "the right" to use eleven surnames, a preposterous number indicating a multiple noble heritage. To make her even more ridiculous, García Márquez supplies her with a golden chamber pot with her family's coat of arms, and a comical nightgown with a hole for supposedly chaste coitus. Both items are ironic combinations of exalted pretensions with those below-the-waist functions that Fernanda finds so embarrassing. Her acts of closing up the house that Ursula had always kept wide open and liquidating Ursula's candy-making business (because it is "undignified") mark the beginning of a new regime in the household.

Although Colonel Aureliano Buendia refuses to accept homage from the government, nevertheless a street in Macondo is named for him; this is another of the written signs by which the community tries to preserve its memories (and like the others, it will fail, as we shall see in the last chapter).

The Mark Of Cain?

The Colonel's seventeen sons, who all return the day of the homage, are a cross-section of the honest, working people of Colombia, representing every region and every color. The indelible ashen cross marked on all their foreheads is perhaps an echo of the mark of Cain, but it will not protect them as Cain's mark was supposed to do.

Once again, a new mode of communications inaugurates a technological and social era in Macondo. Previously, we have seen a foot-trail, a telegraph line, and a boat, each introducing a new social order. Now it is "a frightening thing like a stove pulling a town" (298;210). And, as so often before, the author tells us what is about to happen: "The innocent yellow train that would bring so many uncertainties and evidences, and so many wonders and misadventures, and so many changes, calamities and nostalgias to Macondo." (299;210)

CHAPTER 12: THE COMING OF THE BANANA COMPANY

The focus is on the social changes in the town, which are a simplified version of the real history of many towns in the region in the early twentieth century. A small railroad station with a telephone is built for the train, which brings all kinds of people, vending all kinds of things. A movie house is installed, but the Macondinos dislike what they consider the deceptions of movies, e.g., an actor who is killed in one movie appears alive again in another. This suggests that in some ways the Macondinos are as unsophisticated as they were when Melquiades first visited. But the main change is the arrival of the banana company, which rapidly transforms Macondo "into a camp of wooden houses with zinc roofs." (303;214)

Mr. Herbert's "captive balloon" business occasions a reference to that earlier period of disruption, the arrival of the gypsies with their flying carpets; if the novel were functioning in real time, it is unlikely there would be anyone left alive who remembered those gypsies, who must have passed through seventy or eighty years earlier, but the point is to remind the reader of the repetitions, each with a difference. A separate town is built for the "gringos" (foreigners, especially North Americans). More and more outsiders come to Macondo in "a tumultuous and stormy invasion," and people "put up their houses in whatever bare land they chose without permission from anybody." (304;215) This contrasts to earlier settlers who had always consulted the patriarch Jose Arcadio Buendia before building (third chapter). The extravagant hospitality of the Buendia household, at Aureliano Segundo's insistence, is a memory from the author's childhood; it is effective in the novel because it is precisely opposite the attitude of the gringos (with their fenced-in suburb) and of Fernanda (who wants to close herself and the house uptight).

Typical García Márquez Humor

Remedios the beautiful, oblivious to having caused the death of several men desperate to get a look at her, goes out one day to hang up sheets and, with the sheets, ascends to heaven much the way a popular tradition says that Mary ascended (the ascension is not in the Bible); the detail of the sheets is typical of García Márquez's humor, combining the mundane with the exalted. More comedy is extracted from Fernanda's pious envy and her demand that God return the sheets.

The local authorities are replaced by outsiders, and the local police by "assassins with machetes." (315;224) The fictional massacre of the Aurelianos by police or police agents represents the real deaths of many thousands of campesinos in the renewed outbreak of civil violence early in the century. The colonel then resolves to make a new war to sweep the gringos and their lackeys from the country, but for the Colonel, it is too late: Gerineldo Márquez looks at him compassionately and says, "Ay, Aureliano, I knew you were old, but now I realize that you're much older than you appear." (320;229) The repetition of historical events may be eternal, but human vigor is not.

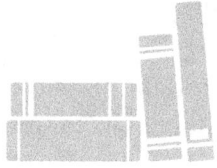

ONE HUNDRED YEARS OF SOLITUDE

TEXTUAL ANALYSIS

CHAPTERS 13-20

CHAPTER 13: THE COLONEL DIES

Jose Arcadio Segundo becomes a foreman in the banana company and has long, private conversations with his great-great-uncle, Colonel Aureliano Buendia: knowledge is being transferred from an older generation of political activist to the younger.

Petra Cotes seems to be entering a second youth while Fernanda is aging rapidly, proving, perhaps, that sex is good for one's health. Aureliano Segundo will henceforth repeatedly move his belongings from Fernanda's (and his own) to Petra's house and back again, showing his deep ambivalence.

The vacation from school of his daughter, Meme, with her seventy-two schoolmates, provides a scene of slapstick comedy and provides another image that will be useful to the novel later on: the seventy-two chamberpots, which after the vacation are stored in Melquiades's old room. Thus, this room of mystery, ironically, becomes known as "the room of the chamberpots."

Colonel Aureliano Buendia, more bitter than ever since his last conversation with Gerineldo Márquez, dies while urinating under the chestnut tree - the mention of urination serving as a reminder that this great, tragic hero is also a very ordinary human, and one who has never tried to polish his rough manners.

This tree is a kind of sacred spot for the family, the place where the colonel's father, Jose Arcadio Buendia, was tied during his madness and where his spirit has dwelt since his death. Thus, the closure of the saga of the colonel recalls that of the saga of the founder.

CHAPTER 14: MEME'S TRAGIC LOVE

This chapter focuses on the succeeding generations of Buendia women, including the birth of a new one, Amaranta Ursula who, as her name implies, will play a key role later on. Aureliano Segundo and Fernanda's older daughter, Meme, after a period of pleasing her mother by playing the clavichord, discovers her father's relationship with Petra Cotes and approves of it. Temperamentally, she resembles the Buendia men more than the earlier women: she is outgoing and fun-loving, like her father, and (like most of the Buendia men) is eager to learn about the wider world. When she begins learning English her father brings her an English encyclopedia; since neither of them can read it, it becomes another magical document to decipher like Melquiades's manuscripts.

Metaphor For Solitude

Death, likewise in the form of a woman, visits Amaranta and tells her to make a shroud and that she will die the day she finishes it. Before she completes this task and dies, Amaranta insists that Ursula examine her to prove to the world that she is still a virgin. Her shroud-making is preparation for the ultimate solitude of death, and her pride that no man has entered her is one more powerful **metaphor** for solitude.

Ursula finally ages, passing her household functions to her granddaughter-in-law, Santa Sofia de la Piedad, in a clear generational succession.

Meme falls in love with Mauricio Babilonia, a mechanic's apprentice in the banana company's workshops; Babilonia, whose name suggests problems of decipherment, has a magical aura in the form of yellow butterflies, suggesting his special destiny (see discussion of characterization, chapter V, page 106). The destiny, we shall learn later, is to father the decipherer of the manuscripts. Despite these fantastic elements, this individualized portrait of a banana worker (the only such portrait in the novel) serves to make the class discrimination against these workers more vivid and believable. It is probably Fernanda's intense class anxiety, her fear of her supposedly noble blood mixing with that of a peon, that provokes her to a violent reaction when she discovers her daughter's affair and causes poor Babilonia's permanent crippling.

CHAPTER 15: MASSACRE OF BANANA WORKERS

The end of the book is foreshadowed in the opening line: "The events that would give the mortal blow to Macondo began to be apparent when the son of Meme Buendia was taken to the house." (365;272) This statement creates suspense, and is also an example of García Márquez's practice of giving the reader the keys to deciphering the text. Without that sentence, the impending "mortal blow" might not be apparent to the reader at all; with it, the reader knows something the characters do not, and so views the struggles of the characters with a measure of **irony** and superiority.

The arrival of Meme's son, named Aureliano by the nuns who delivered him, again excites the class anxieties of Fernanda. Her first impulse is to drown him, but she does not dare - she is cruel, but righteous in her own twisted way. Instead she locks the baby in the colonel's old room, which associates the child's destiny with that great-great-great-uncle. Fernanda's husband and the boy's grandfather, Aureliano Segundo, does not learn of his existence until three years later, when the little child momentarily escapes the room, naked, filthy and "with an impressive sex like a turkey's wattle" (365;272). Moco de pavo, besides its literal meaning of "turkey's wattle," is a purple plant with hanging flowers clustered around one longer one, which explains the image. This plant is a member of the family of amarantaceas, so young Aureliano is thus associated with Amaranta (cf. note in Joset edition, p. 365). The size of Aureliano's sexual organ also associates him with Jose Arcadio, the son of the founder and this child's great-great-grandfather.

García Márquez Borrows From Fuentes

The banana workers' strike closely follows the real historical strike in the region in 1928–29. Jose Arcadio Segundo, a former company foreman, becomes one of the principal agitators, taking up the political causes of Colonel Aureliano Buendia but in the changed context of a mass strike. (His comrade, the Mexican agitator Lorenzo Gavilan, is a character borrowed from Carlos Fuentes' novel, *The Death of Artemio Cruz*. Fuentes had not completed the story of Gavilan, so García Márquez completed it for him.) The authorities' rejection of the workers' demands, on the grounds that the banana company does not have workers because they are not on the payroll, is both historically accurate (this was indeed the government's argument) and another example of the use of words to defend an absurdly false position. It is reminiscent of the politicians' specious arguments to Colonel Aureliano Buendia for ending the war, or the colonel's own words to the man he was about to execute, or Pilar Ternera's card-reading of the past when the town was suffering amnesia. The massacre of the workers at the train station follows historical accounts very closely, even to the words used by the commanding general and the retort of the strikers, although the translator has added the advice as to what to do with "the minute." (378;283) Because García Márquez is working on a larger-than-life scale, however, he greatly inflates the number of casualties, from some dozens (see chapter II, page 15) to three thousand.

Jose Arcadio Segundo's inability to persuade anyone that the massacre actually occurred is a repetition of the **theme** of the struggle for memory against collective amnesia. The inability of the army officer to see Jose Arcadio Segundo, sitting in Melquiades's room, makes clearer than ever that this room is a magical place. Jose Arcadio Segundo also has a sudden insight that reinterprets the career of the colonel: that all the vaunted glories of warfare can be reduced to a single word, "fear."

BRIGHT NOTES STUDY GUIDE

CHAPTER 16: THE DELUGE

Heavy rains begin and will last four years, eleven months and two days - a very precise figure to make an impossibly long event sound possible. The rains are caused by some secret technology of Mr. Brown, a **metaphor** for García Márquez's view that the banana company resulted in nothing but ruin for the town. Aureliano Segundo, for no apparent reason, moves back with his wife and, to kill time, busies himself making repairs in the old house, the first and only Buendia male to concern himself with this task, which in every other case is carried out by women. His grandson Aureliano is now brought into contact with the rest of the family and begins his socialization, although he is not told of his parentage.

Fernanda, furious with the lack of food and her husband's passivity, spends all day insulting him; this develops into the most extraordinary monologue in the book, a three-page, one-sentence tirade in which Fernanda unwittingly reveals all the contradictions of her aspirations and self-pity (395–398; 298–300). Aureliano Segundo then reacts, systematically breaking everything he can in the house, and then throwing a rubberized cape over his shoulders to go out to find some food. This violent gesture recalls the founder and his eldest son, men of few words and violent acts. For the most part, though, the Buendia men are more enchanted by the written word than by action; the colonel was a mixed case, as poet and warrior. Jose Arcadio Segundo, Aureliano Segundo's brother, is now devoting himself entirely to deciphering Melquiades's manuscripts.

Meanwhile little Aureliano and Amaranta Ursula (who is not much older) play in the mud of the patio and catch and torture lizards and toads; their relationship is based on complicity. Ursula, senile and so light they can carry her around easily, has become a fetish doll whom they paint and dress up and whose eyes they very nearly cut out. This odd form of ancestor worship, in which one uses a real ancestor, links the first with the last of the bloodline - for, as we shall see, it will be Aureliano and Amaranta Ursula who finally break Ursula's old taboo.

Aureliano Segundo, who previously had been restoring the house, now undermines its foundations in his desperate search for the gold that Ursula has hidden. Thus, like the colonel before him, he undoes what he has just done.

The deluge has both ruined and purified Macondo. The only inhabitants who remain are those who were there before the banana company's arrival. Aureliano Segundo and Petra Cotes, like earlier characters in the novel, will make a heroic effort to recover what they have lost.

CHAPTER 17: URSULA'S DEATH

When the rains stop, Ursula recovers her lucidity, gets up from bed, and again tries to restore the house, combating the moths and red ants that have been devouring it. When she finds Jose Arcadio Segundo in Melquiades's old room, as mad as his great-grandfather had been under the chestnut tree, and surrounded by the seventy-two excrement-filled chamberpots, he says "Time passes," and she replies, "Yes, but not so much" - realizing as she does so that this is the same dialogue she had once had with her son, the colonel, but with the roles reversed. Again, García Márquez has given us the key to read his text: repetition, but with a change.

In a parallel effort to Ursula's restoration of the house, Aureliano Segundo works very hard with Petra Cotes to recoup their lost fortune. His hand-painting of the raffle tickets, with their odd little symbols, is another document with mystical pretensions, although of course the mystique is much humbler and more mundane than Melquiades's documents.

Another Sign Of The End

Ursula then sinks back into senility and, at the age of 115 or 122 (the family isn't sure), she dies. Since she has been the one constant figure holding the family together and the embodiment of its memory, this is another sign of the coming of the end. This time, the supernatural event accompanying the funeral is more sinister than the rain of flowers at the death of her husband: birds run into walls and kill themselves, so many that it appears to be another plague. This is followed by another strange event, the appearance of "The Wandering Jew," an incident that García Márquez would later expand in the story, "A Very Old Man with Enormous Wings."

That same year Rebeca, a forgotten recluse since the death of her husband, Jose Arcadio, dies. She has long since ceased to play any role in the novel, and seems to be mentioned here only for the purpose of tidying up the story by leaving no major character unaccounted for.

The Macondinos seem again to suffer some of the effects of the plague of amnesia, forgetting important events and who was who. The gypsies who arrive now - another reminder of past epochs - find the town in ruins and the people quite out of touch. They show the inhabitants the same things with which Melquiades had astonished their ancestors: a magnifying glass, magnets, and so on. The new priest who arrives full of enthusiasm is soon infected by the same lassitude as the rest of the town. With Ursula's death, the upkeep of the house is completely neglected, and it looks as decayed as its neighbors.

New Bearer Of Community Memory

Aureliano reaches adolescence ever more aloof and solitary, like his namesake the colonel. He now prefers to remain in the house, where his great-uncle, Jose Arcadio Segundo, has taught him to read and write and has told him about the banana strike and massacre. With the further help of the English encyclopedia that Aureliano Segundo had bought for Meme, young Aureliano becomes learned and, though he has never stepped out of the house, knows many more things than his relatives, including the true cause of the destruction of Macondo: the corruption and repression brought by the banana company. Thus, young Aureliano becomes the new bearer of the town's memory, although he is missing one of the most important data of all: the facts of his own origin.

Aureliano Segundo and his twin brother Jose Arcadio Segundo die at exactly the same moment, and when they are buried the corpses are switched, so that (if Ursula's theory was correct) each regains his true name. This detail simply reinforces the ambiguity García Márquez has created about their respective identities.

CHAPTER 18: DECAY OF MACONDO

Aureliano discovers that the manuscripts are written in Sanskrit, a major breakthrough. After Santa Sofia de la Piedad gives up her efforts to combat the decay of the house and goes off, Aureliano is left alone with his unacknowledged grandmother, Fernanda. Fernanda's madness, like previous cases in the family, is merely an intensification of her old obsessions: she behaves like a queen, dining alone at the head of a table with fifteen empty chairs, linen tablecloths, and candelabra, on the food Aureliano prepares, while the house is falling apart around her. Like a magic princess, when she dies, she is still beautiful despite her age.

When Jose Arcadio (Fernanda's son) returns from Europe four months later, he finds his mother's body perfectly preserved by Aureliano, using Melquiades's formula for vaporizing mercury. This suggests that Aureliano has truly caught the spirit of Melquiades's thinking, because when the founder had tried the same technique to preserve Melquiades's body, he had botched it.

Lone Buendia Homosexual

Jose Arcadio is an arrogant and vain young man and the first and only Buendia homosexual. He is a victim of his mother's and his own deceptions: he had expected to inherit the fortune Fernanda always promised, but this legacy was as much a lie as the seminary studies he had told her he was pursuing.

Aureliano's venture outside the house, for the first time in his life, is a beginning of his coming of age and also an opportunity for the reader to glimpse the changes in Macondo, which has decayed. A true devotee of learning, Aureliano's only interest outside the house is procuring a certain book that Melquiades (or his ghost) has prescribed for him.

Invasion From The Past

Jose Arcadio finds he can share his loneliness with Aureliano, making it easier to bear. Shared solitude is still solitude, however, when each partner is closed against love. The death of the last of the seventeen sons of Colonel Aureliano Buendia is another invasion of the present by the past. Young Aureliano and Jose Arcadio don't know who he is and don't believe his story, and when they turn him away he is instantly killed by the policemen who have been pursuing him for all these years; he is a victim of his relatives' forgetfulness.

It is only after Jose Arcadio is murdered that Aureliano realizes "how much he had begun to love him." (449;346) This awareness always comes too late for the Buendias.

CHAPTER 19: INCEST BETWEEN AMARANTA URSULA AND AURELIANO

Amaranta Ursula arrives in Macondo with her husband, Gaston, a rich, older Fleming who lets her lead him around on a leash - a docility that we cannot imagine in any of the men of Macondo. Cheerful and energetic, Amaranta Ursula combines the restoration fervor of her ancestress Ursula and the strong erotic impulses of Amaranta, though without the latter's bitterness. She sets carpenters, and so on, to restore the house, improving it substantially. She and her husband make love joyously and noisily, greatly arousing Aureliano.

Gaston's hobbies, such as entomology, are pursued with a lack of energy and enthusiasm quite unlike the fanatical Buendias, although he is both imaginative and energetic in sex. When he decides to set up an airmail service and studies the winds and scouts for a good landing site, the Macondinos fear he plans to bring in another banana company. Thus, the memory of that period has not completely faded (although this is contradicted later in the chapter, when other Macondinos deny the existence of Colonel Aureliano Buendia or the massacre of banana workers).

Aureliano meanwhile spends his mornings deciphering the manuscripts and his afternoons in bed with Nigromanta, a young black woman who has recently taken up prostitution and seems to have considerable talent for it. He is repeating the behaviors of that earlier Aureliano, the one who became a colonel. One day he meets four other young habitues of the Catalan's bookstore: Alvaro, German, Alfonso, and Gabriel. He has already encountered a pharmacist's daughter named Mercedes.

Autobiographical Elements

Here, fiction and reality become even more confounded, because (with the probable exception of Nigromanta) all of Aureliano's acquaintances in town are real people whom García Márquez knew in Barranquilla. The Catalan was a professor of literature named Ramon Vinyes, who at one time had owned a bookstore and who (like the Catalan of the novel) eventually went back to Barcelona to spend his last days. Mercedes Barcha, a pharmacist's daughter, is the woman García Márquez married (and the mother of his sons, Gonzalo and Rodrigo, whose names are mentioned in passing, as the names Amaranta Ursula hopes to give her sons). Alvaro Cepeda, German Vargas and Alfonso Fuenmayor were all writer friends of Gabriel García Márquez. The descriptions of these characters in *One Hundred Years of Solitude* are simplified and idealized, like loving caricatures, but immediately recognizable to those who know their prototypes. Because of the presence of these people, and the details of the brothels and bookstores that will appear in this chapter, it is clear that Macondo has been transposed in García Márquez's imagination from the little town of Aracataca, where he spent his childhood, to the coastal city of Barranquilla, where he worked as a young man. (See Chapter II, page 12, for a biography of the author.)

The learned Catalan and the young men, besides being gently drawn memories of García Márquez's real friends, reiterate in a slightly more modern setting the familiar **theme** of the search for knowledge through reading and writing; the Catalan's writings, which we never see, are as cryptic and mysterious as Melquiades's manuscripts, and his bookstore is a treasure house of knowledge. Aureliano's special friend is Gabriel, whose aspirations and subsequent departure for Paris recall the youth of the real Gabriel García Márquez. Gabriel, who is a grandson of Gerineldo Márquez (and thus bears at least one of the author's surnames), is the only person who believes Aureliano's stories of Colonel Aureliano Buendia and of the massacre of the banana workers; the old plague of collective amnesia has infected the others. One can easily imagine that the young Gabriel, grandson of Colonel Márquez, may one day write the stories he hears from Aureliano, which would be a book much like the one we are reading.

Homage To Borges?

The "imaginary little brothel" where Aureliano exhibits his huge phallus appears to be a demonstration of Alvaro's remark that "literature is the best toy invented for making fun of people" (462;357). The author tells us the brothel is imaginary, the characters call it imaginary, and yet there they are, as though the place existed. This is, of course, rather like us, the readers, who are reacting to characters we know do not exist; the book is unmasking its own devices. In this brief scene, García Márquez is toying with the kind of literary paradox associated with the Argentine poet and short-story writer Jorge Luis Borges, and doing it in a very obvious way. The scene may be intended as a **parody** of, or homage to, Borges - or both.

This brothel is soon replaced by one that is more spectacular, if no more fantastic: a zoological brothel named "The Golden Boy," perhaps in memory of all the Aurelianos (aurum, in Latin, means gold). Just what goes on in a zoological brothel is not explained. Do the clients have intercourse with the alligators and other exotic fauna? Or are the animals simply part of the decor? In any case, the ancient Pilar Ternera is the madam, and she recognizes the features (and the destiny) of another Aureliano - the one who became colonel - when she sees this young man. Her long-ago scene with that other Aureliano is repeated with this one, when she recognizes his lovesickness and asks, "Tell me child, who is it?" (470;364) She then explicitly recognizes the organizing principle of the Buendia family destiny, and of this book, in the image of things coming round again and again while the axle is wearing down all the time (470;364). The reader is being prepared for the conclusion, when the axle, or sustaining principle, of the family will decay completely and the wheel stops turning.

The fatal damage to the axle, the self-reproducing capacity of the family, comes when Aureliano finally pounces on Amaranta Ursula. She, after a brief, noiseless struggle (so as not to alert Gaston - she is an accomplice in her own rape), gives in and they make love. Lust springs eternal in Buendia loins, but now it joins two close relatives, breaking Ursula's dreaded taboo.

CHAPTER 20: DESTRUCTION OF MACONDO AND THE BUENDIA LINE

Pilar Ternera dies and is buried like a pagan queen, with all her jewelry and her animals. Like the other burials, hers is appropriate to her character and importance in the novel. Then the Catalan bookseller returns to Barcelona and Aureliano's four young friends all leave Macondo (to idealized versions of the places where the author's real friends did go). The last to leave is Gabriel, who wins a prize from a French magazine and sets out for Paris. García Márquez, who had earlier won a prize for a short story, was sent to Italy and later Paris by the newspaper he worked for. (See Chapter II, page 21, for further parallels.) The town has become so insignificant that he has to flag the train down for it to stop. It has become a place "forgotten even by the birds, where dust and heat had become so tenacious that it took an effort to breathe." (479;371)

"Memory Machine" Fails

When Gaston returns to Brussels, Aureliano and Amaranta Ursula are free to make love all the time, oblivious to the progress of the red ants eating at the foundation of the house. Thus, procreation and destruction are occurring simultaneously. When Amaranta becomes pregnant, Aureliano tries to discover his origins (he fears he may be her brother), but the birth registry in the church is incomplete and the old priest is confused and remembers nothing clearly about the town's history - amnesia again, and the failure of documents to serve as a "memory machine" (Jose Arcadio Buendia's fantasy, in the third chapter). Aureliano and Amaranta Ursula end up accepting the story that, like Moses, he had been found in a basket, "not because they believed it, but because it kept them safe from their terrors." (484;376) Like the readers of a novel, or the young men in the "imaginary brothel" (the nineteenth chapter), they make themselves accomplices in their own deception.

Portrait Of GGM's Wife

The pharmacist's daughter, Mercedes who appears in this and the previous chapter is, without doubt, a portrait of the real Mercedes Barcha, who was the real Gabriel's girlfriend before he went to Europe and is now his wife; these final, playful chapters are full of such personal allusions.

During Amaranta Ursula's pregnancy, she and Aureliano become (like) "a single being" - fulfilling the goal of androgyny of the ancient mystics - and spend all their time in what is left of the house, which only needs a breeze to be knocked down. They lie in bed, unconcerned by the "sublunar explosions of the ants, the clamor of the termites, nor the constant and clear whistling of the weeds growing in the next rooms." (486;378) They are often wakened by the voices of the dead, though: Ursula arguing with "the laws of creation to preserve the bloodline, and Jose Arcadio Buendia looking for the chimerical truth of the great inventions, and Fernanda praying, and Colonel Aureliano Buendia stupefying himself with tricks of wars and little goldfishes, and Aureliano Segundo dying of solitude in the confusion of his revels," because "the dominant obsessions prevail against death." (486;378) This passage appears to be an homage to the garrulous ghosts of the novel *Pedro Paramo*, by Juan Rulfo, which García Márquez read in Mexico shortly before he began writing *One Hundred Years of Solitude*; García Márquez has recalled that in those days he could recite the entire novel from memory (see his "Breves nostalgias sobre Juan Rulfo," in bibliography).

Amaranta bears a healthy male child, "a Buendia of the big ones, robust and willful like the Jose Arcadios, with eyes open and clear-seeing like the Aurelianos, and ready to start the bloodline all over again from the beginning and purify it of its pernicious vices and its vocation of solitude, because it was the only one in a century that had been sired with love." (486;378) But this child, who Aureliano predicts will win thirty-two wars, thus compensating for the thirty-two defeats of the colonel, is in reality the much-predicted baby with a pig's tail, the end of the line.

Pace Quickens

Things move very quickly now. Amaranta Ursula hemorrhages and, to Aureliano's horror, bleeds to death. Distraught, he runs out and wanders about the town, but everyone he knows is dead or gone - having known love, he is again plunged into its opposite, solitude. "Friends are sons of bitches!" he cries (489;380), saying the opposite of what he means - that now, more than ever, he needs his friends. He is the first, and last, Buendia to defeat the solitude within him, but of course it is too late. Everyone else is gone.

Nigromanta, a generous woman, sexually and in other ways, like Pilar Ternera before her, rescues Aureliano from a pool of vomit and tears, and tries to console him. When he remembers the baby, runs back and finds that it is now a dried, swollen piece of flesh being dragged by the ants, he suddenly understands the epigraph of the manuscripts of Melquiades: "The first of the line is tied to a tree and the last is being eaten by ants." (490;381) This is the first mention of an epigraph, which here suddenly appears to be very important. Its function in the story is to provide Aureliano with the key for deciphering the rest of Melquiades's text.

Did Melquíades Write The Novel?

Aureliano runs to the manuscripts and begins reading furiously, finding in them the whole history of the family. He skips ahead to find his own history and future and reads of his own destruction and the destruction of Macondo just as these occur. The reader (Aureliano) is the same as the one who is being read. The other readers, you and I, are suddenly hit with the possibility that the entire novel has been a fiction created by Melquiades, who is, of course, a fiction created by García Márquez. "Literature is the best toy ever invented to make fun of people," the author has already warned us; in fiction, there may be imaginary things inside imaginary things. To further confuse the boundaries, these last two chapters have been filled with real people under their own names (Alvaro, Gabriel, Mercedes), as though the author's intention was to subvert the fictional process itself.

A Final Pun

As the wind carries off Macondo, the Buendias and the author's twenty-year obsession with the stories of his childhood, we are told that for "the bloodlines condemned to one hundred years of solitude" there is no "second opportunity on earth." (493;383) This leaves us with a final pun, because the sentence could also mean there is no second chance for those who have been condemned to reading - or the one who was condemned to writing - *One Hundred Years of Solitude*. In that case, there will be no sequel; García Márquez has finally said everything he had to say about Macondo.

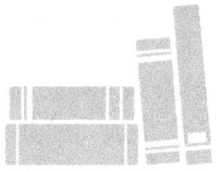

ONE HUNDRED YEARS OF SOLITUDE

ANALYSIS OF CHARACTERS

The central character is the town of Macondo, whose history from its founding in the early nineteenth century to its apparent destruction in the mid-twentieth century is told through the lives of the Buendias and their mates. What follows is a discussion of García Márquez's general techniques of characterization, followed by a discussion of the more important individual characters, arranged by generation.

TECHNIQUES OF CHARACTERIZATION

The names of characters often suggest something about their personalities, either straightforwardly or ironically. For example, Prudencio Aguilar is neither "prudent" nor "eagle-like" (aguila means "eagle" in Spanish).

Repetition of names and behaviors is another technique of characterization. Certain character types, e.g., the contemplative, stubborn man, or the impetuous, forceful man, the patient and nurturing woman, and so on, are represented by more than one individual in the several generations of the Buendia family. All the Jose Arcadios, for example, are assumed to have at least some of the traits of the original Jose Arcadio Buendia (impetuous and forceful), and all the Aurelianos have something in common with Colonel Aureliano Buendia (tendency toward solitude and contemplation). The repetitions are not exact, but the use of similar names is one way to suggest more about a character than is actually said. There are also repetitions of particular behaviors, for example, secluding oneself in a room for experiments or study.

Some characters have characteristic signs to identify them. Examples include Pilar Ternera's laugh, Colonel Aureliano Buendia's solitary look, Aureliano Segundo's extravagance, Fernanda's continual muttering, and so on.

Physical descriptions are used sparingly, letting the reader fill in the details beyond such generalities as "skinny" or "fat," "beautiful," "huge." An exception is made for Colonel Aureliano Buendia, who seems to be drawn from an especially clear mental image of the author's, as though copied from a photograph.

Some of the more spectacular individuals are characterized by the effects they have on others. The founder, Jose Arcadio Buendia, is obeyed unquestioningly by his companions; his son Colonel Aureliano Buendia inspires respect and fear; Amaranta deliberately manipulates men's lust; Remedios the beautiful creates paroxysms of erotic passion.

Occasionally, a character can be identified by a characteristic type of speech. Jose Arcadio Buendia (the founder) is given to harsh, short, judgmental declarations: "The world is round, like an orange!" Ursula speaks sternly, also in short sentences. Fernanda del Carpio goes on at great length, in a vocabulary reminiscent of the sixteenth century (Spain's "Century of Gold" in literature), especially in her magnificent, one-sentence, three-page monologue. Jose Arcadio Segundo speaks very simply and directly. Unfortunately, some of these subtleties (particularly the antiquated vocabulary of Fernanda) are almost impossible to convey in translation, although Gregory Rabassa has made a noble effort.

A. First Generation

Jose Arcadio Buendia

Jose Arcadio Buendia (ho-Say ar-Kah-dee-o bwen-Dee-a). Buendia is literally "Good day," perhaps suggesting the goodheartedness and simplicity of these people. The name Arcadio comes from Arcadia, a mountainous district of Greece which, since the Roman poet Virgil, has symbolized an ideal pastoral world, where man and nature lived in harmony - much like Macondo in its early period. This Jose Arcadio Buendia, the founder of the family and of the town of Macondo, is physically powerful and energetic and single-minded to the point of obsession in pursuit of his extravagant projects, and he ultimately goes mad. His namesakes will likewise tend to be physically big, powerful, single-minded and outgoing men - until the fifth generation.

Ursula Iguaran

Ursula Iguaran (Ur-su-la ee-gwa-Rahn). The long-suffering matriarch of the clan bears the name of a twelfth-century British saint who, according to legend, was martyred with eleven thousand virgins by the Huns. (It may or may not be relevant to her incest obsession that Ursula is also the name of the pig-woman in Ben Jonson's 1614 comedy, Bartholomew Fair.) Her unusual family name, Iguaran, was in reality García Márquez's grandmother's maiden name. Small, hardworking, and practical, she keeps the family together while her husband and (later) her sons are engaged in wild, impractical projects. It is she who orders the house improved and enlarged and personally supervises construction, for example. Her character is also one of the things holding the novel together, since she alone of all the characters is present from the first chapter to almost the end. She dies senile and blind, but struggling to the end to preserve the family.

Pilar Ternera

Pilar Ternera (pee-Lar ter-Neh-ra). Her last name is very suggestive of her personality: a ternera is a calf, and the word is also very close to ternura, Spanish for "tenderness." Pilar's role will be as comforter and sometimes bedmate to the Buendia males. Jilted by a lover as a girl, she keeps looking for Mr. Right but in the meanwhile takes any number of Mr. Wrongs to bed, and symbolizes sexual generosity. Her ridiculous efforts to tell the future and even the past from cards, always getting things hopelessly confused, is a comic commentary on the futility of trying to get the truth from reading any literary work, including (presumably) this novel. She will live even longer than Ursula, and is last seen at the age of one hundred forty-five as the madam of a marvelous zoological brothel visited by the last male of the Buendia tribe.

Melquiades

Melquiades (mel-Kee-ah-dess). The name of this globetrotting gypsy, possessor of an immense store of medieval and

Renaissance learning, may have been suggested by Melchizedek, a celebrated combination of priest and king mentioned in Genesis and again in Psalms. His physical description is very elaborate and detailed, down to the strange, old-fashioned garments he wears; he is something exotic, outside the world of Macondo, and thus in a position to comment on it. He also returns from the dead when he is needed, much the way an old book comes to life when a new reader discovers it, and cures the townspeople of their amnesia plague; surely a reference to the importance of knowledge to retaining the collective past of a people. Melquiades also stands for authorship - some critics suggest he is the "author" of *One Hundred Years of Solitude* - as the author of the "parchments" that are the key to the history of the Buendias and of Macondo.

Prudencio Aguilar

Prudencio Aguilar. (pru-Den-see-o ah-ghee-Lar). As mentioned above, the name is ironic: he is neither "prudent" nor "eagle-like" (aguila means "eagle" in Spanish), foolishly taunting the far more powerful Jose Arcadio Buendia. He introduces a favorite **theme** of García Márquez's, that the dead also suffer until they reach a "death within death," a final death. This foreshadows the ghosthood of Melquiades.

B. Second Generation

Jose Arcadio

Born to Jose Arcadio Buendia (senior) and Ursula Iguaran, on their trek through the wilderness to found Macondo, he is a transitional figure. He is big, strong, and willful like his father, but "lacking imagination." He is also unlike his father in that he is completely free of any sense of communal obligation. When Pilar Ternera, with whom he has had his first sexual experience, tells him she is pregnant, he runs off with a band of gypsies. He later blithely seizes his neighbors' lands to become the town's biggest landowner, in a complete reversal of his father's policy of strictly equal distribution of land. This character represents pure animal vitality, unmitigated by any sense of morality. He symbolizes the breakdown of the patriarchal values represented by his father, but without the cynicism or worldliness that will characterize Macondo at a later stage.

Aureliano

Aureliano (ow-reh-lee-Ah-no). The name comes from the Latin word for gold (aurum); Aureliano Buendia will become a goldsmith. The second son of the Buendias and the first human to be born in Macondo, he is withdrawn and pensive and can sense things that are about to occur; later Aurelianos will also have these traits. García Márquez makes clear that the ability to foresee things is of little practical use, because of the difficulty of correctly reading one's premonitions. Thus, this gift of Aureliano's is another commentary on how truth eludes a reader of a text. Actually, as a boy Aureliano is an assiduous reader of Melquiades's manuscripts, but gets nothing out of them. Later, as Colonel Aureliano Buendia, he leads thirty-two armed uprisings and loses them all. He represents not only the futility of wars but, more importantly to García Márquez, the terrible isolation of a man with power: at the height of his power, he has a chalk circle drawn around him and refuses to let anyone, even his mother, approach. In retirement, he underscores the futility of his life, first by burning all the poetry he has written, then by repeatedly making, melting down, and remaking little goldfishes. He is one of the most solitary characters in this whole family of solitaries.

Amaranta

Amaranta (ah-ma-Ran-ta). The name of the Buendias daughter and youngest child leads García Márquez to a play on the Spanish word, amamantar, to suckle (108:41), but an association with amargura, "bitterness," seems more appropriate to her character. (Amarantina and amaranto are both flowering plants, with no obvious relationship to her character; García Márquez probably chose the name for its sound.) Amaranta goes through life sexually enticing men and boys (including her nephew Aureliano Jose), but rejecting them when they propose marriage or get close to intercourse. The first time she does this is with Pietro Crespi, who is driven to suicide; her only visible reaction is to cripple her own hand by holding it in a flame. This suggests that her emotions are so thoroughly turned inward that she can only express grief through self-punishment. Given García Márquez's very positive view of sex, her stubborn defense of her virginity to her dying day can be read as another form of self-deprivation or self-punishment. She is one of the loneliest of all these lonely characters.

Pietro Crespi

Pietro Crespi (Pyeh-tro Kress-pee), the Italian dancing master, is characterized by his fancy, almost effeminate dress and his overly delicate manners. The last name comes from crespo, which in both Italian and Spanish describes curly hair.

Rebeca

Rebeca (reh-Beh-ka), an orphan of unknown origin brought up as a daughter by the Buendias, secretly eats dirt and lime from the walls and is the first to come down with the plague of insomnia. Her namesake in the Bible, the wife of Isaac, is childless for many years before she gives birth to the twins, Jacob and Esau; this Rebeca is childless all her life. After Amaranta sabotages her engagement to Pietro Crespi, she discovers the exuberant joy of sex with her foster brother Jose Arcadio, but after his death reveals her true vocation for solitude: she locks herself up in her house until the town forgets her. Her solitude makes her a true Buendia.

C. Third Generation

Arcadio

Arcadio, illegitimate son of Jose Arcadio (junior) and Pilar Ternera, is selfish and vigorous. Left in command of the town by his uncle Aureliano, he is an abusive, pompous martinet who so enrages his grandmother Ursula that she storms out of the house to give him a spanking in front of his troops. His character presents a simplified and comical example of the arrogance of power that will be presented more fully and tragically in the career of his uncle, Colonel Aureliano Buendia. Arcadio is a vital link in the family chain: the final generation of Buendias will all be descended from his union with Santa Sofia de la Piedad.

Santa Sofia de la Piedad

Santa Sofia de la Piedad (Sahn-ta so-Fee-ah deh lah pee-eh-Dahd) was the name of a Christian church in Constantinople

(Istanbul) which later became a mosque and is now a museum of Byzantine art; García Márquez may be using the name simply to remind us once again of the mysterious beliefs of the East, so that we do not lose sight of the teachings of the gypsy Melquiades. This character is hardly developed at all and really is practically invisible in the Buendia household, even though she is the mother of Arcadio's three children and, after Ursula's death, the only person who tries to keep the house and family together. Never a true Buendia, in extreme old age she announces that the house is too much for her and goes off to live with a remnant from her own family, a sister; her nonmembership in the Buendia family is shown by the fact that nobody tries either to stop her or help her.

Aureliano Jose

Aureliano Jose, son of Aureliano and Pilar Ternera, as a boy is constantly stimulated sexually by his aunt, Amaranta. He goes off to fight for the Liberal cause in Central America but returns, hoping to make love to Amaranta - who rejects him. Thus he serves both to underscore the idealistic side of the Buendias' revolutionary activities, and to sustain the novel's **theme** of incest. Proud and independent, he is murdered by a Conservative officer when he refuses to let himself be frisked.

The Seventeen Aurelianos

The seventeen Aurelianos, sons of Colonel Aureliano Buendia by as many mothers, represent a cross-section of the colors and types of the population of the country. They are hardly characterized individually at all, but as a group are all simple, hardworking, and good-natured, which is the way García

Márquez generally depicts the working class. Mysteriously, the ash the priest uses to mark their foreheads on Ash Wednesday is indelible, a mark which does not protect them (like the mark of Cain) but instead becomes a target. All but Aureliano Amador are assassinated, shot or stabbed through the cross on the forehead, in a single day; the sole survivor reappears years later, still pursued by police, and is killed on the threshold of the Buendia house, where he has sought refuge.

D. Fourth Generation

Colonel Aureliano Buendia leaves no grandchildren (at least, not that we know about), but his brother's son Arcadio and Santa Sofia de la Piedad have three children.

Remedios

Remedios (reh-Meh-dee-os) "the beautiful" is the eldest, as innocent as she is beautiful. We are not told what she looks like, only that she is "beautiful:" let the reader supply his or her own notion of beauty. She is described primarily by the impact she has on others, especially the men who fall so hopelessly in love with her that they either die or turn into panting beasts. Her unreality is dramatized when she becomes nearly transparent and, in a comic variation on the legendary ascension of Mary, rises to heaven with the sheets flapping around her.

Aureliano Segundo

Aureliano Segundo (seh-Goon-do) and Jose Arcadio Segundo are identical twins who apparently switch identities in childhood, because the one called Aureliano Segundo is more like the Jose Arcadios of the family - outgoing, spontaneous, energetic - and his brother is more like the Aurelianos - withdrawn, thoughtful, serious.

Jose Arcadio Segundo

Jose Arcadio Segundo (or the one so-called) becomes a strike organizer for the banana workers in the North American fruit company. When the strikers are massacred by troops, he survives and witnesses the long train carrying the corpses to the sea; he is one of those Buendias responsible for carrying the memories of the clan and the town. He goes mad when no one will believe his story - because memory, confronting collective amnesia, is a very heavy burden - and locks himself in Melquiades's old room, remembering and trying to decipher the manuscripts.

Aureliano Segundo

Aureliano Segundo, with the help of his concubine Petra Cotes, becomes a rich animal breeder, throwing raucous parties for his neighbors and entertaining them with his accordion. He symbolizes the prosperity and profligacy of those years during and just after the First World War. He falls in love with and marries Fernanda del Carpio, a very different kind of woman from Petra, and thereafter divides his life between the two women and the two households. He is depicted as a psychologically healthy bourgeois who loves sex and is also very affectionate toward his concubine, his wife, and his children, and who struggles to provide for them after economic disaster.

Fernanda Del Carpio

Fernanda del Carpio (fehr-Nahn-da del Kar-pee-o) is an extremely pious (or superstitious) ignorant woman from the part of Colombia that García Márquez likes least, the cold, austere mountains near Bogota, where (according to him) everybody wears black and is generally grim. The author makes her especially ridiculous by having her claim the right to use eleven surnames - suggesting an exceptionally complex noble lineage - and as using a gold-plated chamber pot embossed with the family crest. Her first name is a version of Fernando, the name of several Spanish kings (including the one who married Isabel and cosponsored Columbus' voyages). Bernardo del Carpio is a Spanish mythical hero of many romantic **epics** from Spain's Golden Age (sixteenth century) and earlier. Besides her names, García Márquez gives her a vocabulary that often suggests a mentality out of the Middle Ages. Her character is the sharpest possible contrast to two recurrent Buendia traditions, generosity toward strangers and frank speech: as soon as she gets the upper hand Fernanda orders the house sealed, and she uses such euphemisms for ordinary bodily functions that the Buendias cannot even understand her. She does terribly cruel things out of her superstitious ignorance and sexual repression, causing the crippling of her daughter's lover and the insanity of her daughter, and locking up her grandson in a room, but still García Márquez treats her with sympathy. Her correspondence with the invisible doctors, for example, is funny but also terribly sad, showing her incapacity to deal rationally with a fairly simple physical problem (a collapsed uterus).

Petra Cotes

Petra Cotes (Peh-tra Ko-tess) is followed in the novel from her sexually attractive youth to a noble and generous old age, sacrificing herself for her lover, Aureliano Segundo, and then for her lover's widow, Fernanda. The name (from the Greek for "rock") is from García Márquez's family: he did have an Aunt Petra. She is a kind of fertility goddess, making Aureliano Segundo's animals multiply and his fields yield bumper crops, even though she herself never bears a child.

E. Fifth Generation

Meme

Meme (Meh-meh) is the nickname of Renata (reh-Nah-ta) Remedios, elder daughter of Fernanda and Aureliano Segundo. Renata comes from the word for queen, and reflects her mother's aristocratic pretensions; Remedios is the Buendias' way of remembering the two earlier women of that name in the family. Meme is a cheerful, carefree girl who is her father's favorite. She conforms outwardly to her mother's demands (studying at a nuns' school, learning the harpsichord), but has a wild, rebellious spirit that emerges when she invites her schoolmates home for vacation and later when she falls in love with a peon and continues to see him despite her mother's prohibition. She becomes the mother of the last surviving Buendia.

Mauricio Babilonia

Mauricio Babilonia (mow-Ree-see-o ba-bee-Lo-nee-ah), is a mechanic's apprentice for the banana company and lover of Meme (above) and father of her son, Aureliano. His last name, suggesting the indecipherability of the Tower of Babel, will be more apt for his son than for his own role. Mauricio is characterized by his odor of oil and the yellow butterflies that surround him wherever he goes, a kind of living halo that, in the tradition of heroic myths, suggests some special destiny for him. This destiny is to father the story's final hero, decipherer Aureliano. The playful-sacred image of the yellow butterflies becomes a kind of curse after Mauricio is shot and paralyzed and the butterflies will not leave him alone.

Jose Arcadio

Jose Arcadio, son of Fernanda and Aureliano Segundo, is first described as a baby, "languid and whiny, with no trace of a Buendia." (258) He is reared by Fernanda and his great-great-grandmother Ursula to become the Pope, and while still a boy is sent to Rome. He returns years later, after both parents have died, believing (because his mother had told him so) that he would inherit great wealth; he has done no serious studying in Rome, religious or otherwise, and has become a decadent, foppish homosexual, bored with Macondo and desperate when he realizes the legacy was another of his mother's myths. He is the first, and last, homosexual Buendia, a weakling with no especially admirable traits; giving him the name of the original founder of Macondo, the decisive and forceful patriarch, is a way of suggesting how far the family has degenerated. Still, García Márquez treats him sympathetically as a poor victim of other people's absurdly unrealistic expectations (that he would become Pope and that he would inherit great wealth). A true Buendia in at least one respect, he is unable to love and is ultimately murdered by his juvenile sex partners whom he has spurned and beaten.

Amaranta Ursula

Amaranta Ursula is the youngest child of Fernanda and Aureliano Segundo and the last woman of the family. She unites in her names and in her character the opposite extremes of Buendia womanhood. Like her great-great-aunt Amaranta, she is impelled toward sex and incest. Like her great-great-grandmother Ursula, she will strive to restore the house and to prolong the bloodline. Her failure in both enterprises, restoring the house and prolonging the family, can be read as the result of the collision of these conflicting tendencies in the family. She makes love with her nephew Aureliano and bears the last Buendia baby, the child with a pig's tail who fulfills Ursula's prophecy of the fate of incestuous unions.

F. Sixth Generation

Aureliano

Aureliano is the illegitimate son of Meme Buendia and Mauricio Babilonia, and thus is the nephew of Amaranta Ursula. Babylonia, of course, was the ancient near eastern empire best remembered in the Bible for the tower of Babel, symbol of the incomprehensibility of foreign languages; Aureliano Babilonia will be the first in the family to decipher the strange language of Melquiades's manuscripts. Like Amaranta Ursula, he unites opposite characteristics of the family. Like Jose Arcadio, junior, his great-great-grandfather, he has huge sex organs and enormous potency, and enjoys carousing with his friends. Like his great-great-greatuncle Colonel Aureliano Buendia and his greatuncle Jose Arcadio Segundo, who becomes his teacher, he also has a very strong need to be alone in his room to study and think. He becomes the only surviving bearer of the memories of the history of the town and of the family, the only one who remembers that there was a Colonel Aureliano Buendia who raised thirty-two armed rebellions and lost them all, and that there was a strike in which three thousand workers were killed. And, as mentioned above, he is finally the decoder of the manuscripts, aided by the ghost of Melquiades. He ties everything up in this novel: memory, incest, solitude, reading, and prophecy. It is Aureliano who makes friends with a group of young intellectuals, all bearing the names of old friends of García Márquez and one named Gabriel. Aureliano even meets the ancient Pilar Ternera, now the madam of an extravagant brothel. And, by making love to his young aunt Amaranta Ursula and impregnating her, he becomes the fulfiller as well as the decoder of the prophecy made at the beginning of the book.

G. Seventh And Final Generation

The Son With A Pig's Tail

The son with a pig's tail is given no name. Born to Amaranta Ursula and her nephew Aureliano, he is the offspring of the most incestuous relationship in the family and is also (according to the narrator) the first Buendia conceived in love - a puzzling statement, since his father, Aureliano (Babilonia) would also seem to have been conceived in love. He appears to be well-equipped to father a new generation (that is, he has big sex organs and is born healthy and vigorous), but the pig-tailed baby is in reality the last of the line, killed and dragged off by the same ants that have been undermining the house.

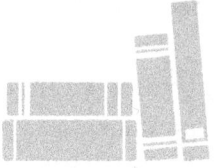

ONE HUNDRED YEARS OF SOLITUDE

CRITICAL AND POLITICAL REPUTATION

One Hundred Years of Solitude is one of those rare novels that "simultaneously made the best-seller lists and precipitated a critical industry." (Janes 1981:48) Thousands of articles and hundreds of books on this novel have appeared, including such oddities as a Gramscian analysis of the history of Macondo (Vadillo, 1984; Antonio Gramsci, 1891–1937, was an Italian revolutionary and philosopher), a Hegelian interpretation of the novel's "solitude" (Farias, 1981), and a study of the Buendias' concept of God (Verges, 1973). The book seems to have something for everybody. There are even book-length studies of the book-length studies (see, for example, Abenoza, 1979), and no end to this process is in sight.

Even before it was published, Mexican novelist Carlos Fuentes (having read the first chapters) hailed the uncompleted book as a masterpiece, and he was soon joined in this opinion by other major Latin American writers, including the Argentinian Julio Cortazar and the Cuban Guillermo Cabrera Infante -who complained that his wife read *One Hundred Years of Solitude* twice before taking up Cabrera's own *Tres tristes tigres* (Three Trapped Tigers), published the same year. Mario Vargas Llosa, a Peruvian novelist eight years younger than García Márquez but already immensely popular, then went much further; he produced a 664-page book on García Márquez which remains the authoritative biography of the years up to 1969. As *One Hundred Years of Solitude* began to appear in translation, it generated almost as much excitement among writers and readers abroad, although there are relatively few book-length studies in English.

"... NOW THE WHOLE STORY"

Mario Benedetti, noted Uruguayan poet, essayist, and novelist, writing in 1967, concluded that *One Hundred Years of Solitude* transformed all of García Márquez's previous fiction (which Benedetti admired) into a mere "draft of this exceptional novel," having served as a "springboard for the great imaginative leap. Apparently each of the previous books was a fragment of the history of Macondo ... and this now is the whole story." (Benedetti, 1969:18) The Macondo that had appeared earlier may have been an image of the entire country of Colombia, but in this work "Macondo is approximately all of Latin America; it is tentatively the world," and the history of the Buendias is "also that of Man, who has had not one hundred but thousands of years of solitude." (Benedetti:19) Macondo, he argued, was more "real" than those other well-known fictional places, Faulkner's *Yoknapatawpha County* and *Onetti's Santa Maria*, because the "things" in Macondo (the colonel's umbrella and watch in *No One Writes to the Colonel*, the billiard balls in "En este pueblo no hay ladrones," and so on) are more than mere reference points, but are summary "data of consciousness" of the town's life. Benedetti appears to mean that García Márquez makes these things the objects of intense concern to the characters and so they serve to define their consciousness. He also notes that in all of García's works (which he admires greatly) there are seldom scenes of "unbridled violence," but that violence is a felt, off-stage presence (Benedetti, 1967:13).

NO MORE "FOLIAGE"

Carballo (1967) was impressed by the "austerity" of García Márquez's style, meaning that the sentences were relatively simple and unadorned with what García Márquez himself had called the "rhetorical foliage" that plagued much Latin American prose and his own earlier writing. The "foliage" referred mainly to an abundance of adjectives and adverbs, a Faulknerian exuberance that the author had deliberately purged from his writing.

TOO ELITIST? TOO "LITERARY?"

Carballo also raised a question that would frequently be heard from critics on the political left: "up to what point should the novel, and all the other literary genres, reflect the objective conditions, in this case underdevelopment, or to what point is it legitimate ... to go further and give the readers a technical and stylistic image in accord with what has been happening in the most advanced laboratories of the countries that live and enjoy the advantages of the twentieth century." In other words, was García Márquez's writing too elitist, or too "literary," for the Third World? To his credit, Carballo thought not, agreeing with what he takes to be García Márquez's position "that economic and political underdevelopment do not have to result necessarily in a technically conformist novel nor in one that ignores the historical context of the continent" (Carballo, 1967:36). He calls *One Hundred Years of Solitude* "a perfect novel" because its "structure, story, characters and style fully achieve their object" (Carballo:37).

Julio Ortega argued that "the notorious success of *One Hundred Years of Solitude* is rooted in the fact that its obvious quality is also a long praise of the reader. It is a novel that demands and obtains the best of each reader... . And this is because *One Hundred Years of Solitude* shatters reason, excites fantasy, makes sensitivity transparent, demands humor, convokes piety." The novel is also effective, according to Ortega, because the (Latin American) reader recognizes in it his or her country's own past, "because the world and the time that this novel relates is closed, concluded. The history of Macondo is the history of the past." (Ortega, 1968:74)

The Uruguayan journalist and critic Angel Rama was an early admirer of García Márquez's work, even before *One Hundred Years* was published. On the author's treatment of the **theme** of violence, what impressed Rama was not that it usually took place "off-stage" (Benedetti's point), but that the characters' motives for violence were explained by their "social context." Thus the characters are not simply heroes or villains, but respond to specific material conditions and, like real people, generally are "not fully conscious of the significance of their acts." (Rama, 1969:115)

"A LITERARY EARTHQUAKE"

Mario Vargas Llosa has described the novel as "a literary earthquake in Latin America," not only recognized as a masterpiece by the critics but snatched up by the reading public so rapidly that at one point new editions were coming out at the rate of one per week. This success is mainly owing to the book's three main virtues, he argues. The first of these is that it is a "'total' novel, in the line of those insanely ambitious creations that aspire to compete with reality as an equal, facing it with an image of a qualitatively equal vitality, vastness and complexity." Second, it has a "plural nature," simultaneously being opposite things: traditional and modern, localist and universal, imaginary and realistic. Third, "perhaps the most mysterious of its virtues" is "its unlimited accessibility, that is, its quality of being within reach, with different but abundant prizes for all, of the intelligent reader and the imbecile, of the complicated and the simple spirit, of the refined who savor prose, contemplate the architecture and decipher the symbols of a fiction, and of the impatient who only pays attention to the crude anecdote." (1969:126–127)

What Vargas Llosa means by a "total" novel remains somewhat obscure. He is probably referring to the sensation many readers get from the book, that it is much bigger than it is, because it alludes to events larger than Colombia, larger even than Latin America. To a certain kind of reader, the book may seem to be all-encompassing because that reader picks up García Márquez's cues and completes the references from his or her own memories and imagination.

THE FICTION-WRITER AS A "GOD-KILLER"

Vargas Llosa then went on to develop these ideas in a 664-page book on García Márquez, subtitled "history of a deicide." It was quite a surprising thing for one very successful young novelist (Vargas Llosa is eight years younger than García Márquez) to devote so much energy to promoting a rival, but it appears that the Peruvian was interested for his own reasons in exploring the process of fictional creation, using his Colombian colleague as a case study. Unlike García himself, who has said, "I never talk about literature, because I don't know what it is," Vargas Llosa has devoted much attention to discussing and analyzing literature. His explanation for his title is that every fiction writer is a "deicide," a God-killer, because he destroys the given reality to create his own, usurping and supplanting God.

According to Vargas Llosa, a writer also struggles against personal "demons" - images and experiences from his past that assume an almost obsessive importance. García Márquez's "demons" are almost all to be found in his childhood in Aracataca, which Vargas Llosa details in what remains the most informative available account of García Márquez's life up to about 1969.

Angel Rama took offense at Vargas Llosa's quasi-religious vocabulary ("demons" and "deicide") in a lengthy review of the Peruvian's book, and the latter rebutted Rama, who then replied, and so on. The curious book that resulted, *García Márquez y la problematica de la novela* ("García Márquez and the 'problematic' of the novel," Vargas Llosa and Rama, 1973), sheds very little light on García Márquez but does illustrate the passions his work aroused.

| A PATH THAT NONE COULD FOLLOW?

Regina Janes' elegant and witty *Gabriel García Márquez: Revolutions in Wonderland* (1981) is one of the few book-length studies in English. Janes analyzes the evolution of García Márquez's writing technique as well as his personal and political concerns, tracing the development of **themes** and techniques through his short stories and early novels that made possible the great breakthrough of *One Hundred Years of Solitude*. She echoes Vargas Llosa's argument that, with *One Hundred Years*, García

Márquez had settled accounts with his boyhood memories (what Vargas Llosa calls his "demons"), but what is more interesting to Janes is that García had resolved certain technical problems of how to represent the flow of time, the unreliability of memory, and so on. Then he was ready to move on to other kinds of writings. She says of the stories of *La candida Erendira y su abuela desalmada*, his next work, that he was "writing his way out of *One Hundred Years of Solitude*" and getting set for *Autumn of the Patriarch*, which she calls a "perfect" fit of means and ends. (*Chronicle of a Death Foretold* had not yet appeared.) She suggests that García Márquez may actually have done a disservice to his fellow Latin American writers, because he had blazed a path that none could follow - as though he had not only created, but simultaneously exhausted the new techniques. According to her, unlike earlier great modernist writers, "García Márquez has not, or so it seems to me, opened up new possibilities for other writers; rather, he seems to have closed off certain avenues, though he may of course have imitators. Certain aspects of his rhetoric are, like Milton's, dangerously imitable, and the end he has accomplished, the representation of a bizarre, complex, and complete world, tempting." (Janes, 1981:49) However, anyone familiar with the works of younger "magic realists," such as Venezuela's amazing Luis Britto García, will find Janes' prediction overly pessimistic.

GARCÍA MÁRQUEZ'S "HETEROGLOSSIA"

Another useful work in English is Raymond L. Williams' study (1984), which includes an extensive annotated bibliography of García Márquez's publications, the translations, and much of the critical literature. With regard to *One Hundred Years of Solitude*, Williams is particularly interested in the contrasting levels of discourse - the style of Melquiades' manuscripts versus government decrees, Fernanda's rantings, comic conversations, and so on - which, following Mikhail Bakhtin, he calls "heteroglossia."

The influence of William Faulkner on García Márquez's work, especially the similarity between Faulkner's fictional Yoknapatawpha County in Mississippi and García's Macondo, has been noted by many critics, and has been acknowledged by García Márquez himself. Ernesto Volkening (1963) was perhaps the first to make this point about García Márquez's earlier books, long before *One Hundred Years* had been written. The North American author Harley D. Oberhelman (1980) has treated this question in detail. In a 1981 *The Paris Review* interview, García Márquez remarks that the Faulknerian influence has been exaggerated, that it was really "a coincidence: I had simply found material that had to be dealt with in the same way that Faulkner had treated similar material." However, there is no question that he had read and been impressed by Faulkner.

There is also a collection in *English of Critical Perspectives on Gabriel García Márquez* (Shaw and Vera-Godwin, 1986). Here, Michael Palencia-Roth compares Christopher Columbus' diary to García's attempt, in Autumn of the Patriarch, to reproduce, by reversing the perspective, the wonder of the "natives" discovery of Columbus. Robert L. Sims analyzes "Matriarchal and Patriarchal Patterns" in *One Hundred Years of Solitude* and the other novels, while John Incledon examines the relationship of "Writing and Incest." He concludes that "the destruction of Macondo, rather than the end of a delightful world of magical **realism**, points to the foreseeable end of the cultural and ideological heritage of Spain in the New World. The novel is revolutionary in a profound sense." Rather than Bakhtin, Sims looks to Jacques Derrida's deconstruction technique for an analytical model.

"TIME IN ITS REALITY"

In the same collection, Mary C. Pinard focuses on time and solitude in *One Hundred Years of Solitude*. In English, solitude means the "state of being alone," but in *One Hundred Years of Solitude*

> soledad... as experienced by certain characters, is a psychological state that is personal and exclusive of society wherein spatial or clock time, considered as a quantity of change measured by motion, does not usually exist." It is clear as early as the first sentence of the book that García Márquez is weaving his plot and characters into overlapping worlds of clock time (divisible and measurable) and time in its reality (continuous, indivisible) ... Characters move in and out of solitude: they may consciously choose it to complete a task in private, or solitude may be imposed from the outside by certain events (insomnia, plague), by Nature (four years of incessant rain), or by other characters (Melquiades). Characters outside of solitude are acutely aware of those in solitude because they seem remote, out of the stream of things, essentially unreachable. They appear to be outside clock time. (Pinard, 1986:65)

Morton P. Levitt makes this interesting observation about the point of view of *One Hundred Years of Solitude*:

> There are few explanations, and those that there are come not from outside with certainty - from the omniscient author, that is - but from within the community, and they add thereby to the uncertainty of what may be accepted as real and what may remain something else. Fully explained, such phenomena as

> the mysterious lampoons [in the earlier novel, In Evil Hour] and motion pictures would become further examples of simple exotica in a strange, distant, isolated town - and nothing more; left as they are, seen solely through the eyes of some resident or even of the town as a whole, largely ambiguous, promising of metaphor, they may reach beyond the normal bounds of the Realistic and toward the universal. (Levitt, 1986:76)

As an example of such an ambiguous, exotic event, he mentions discovery of the galleon (in the first chapter of One Hundred Years).

PAZ: "HIS IDEAS ARE POOR ... SLOGANS"

There are many people who criticize García Márquez for his politics, including (lately) Vargas Llosa and the Mexican poet Octavio Paz. For example, Paz has said, "I don't reproach García Márquez for using his skill as a writer to defend his ideas. I reproach him because his ideas are poor. There is an enormous difference between what I do and what García Márquez does. I try to think and he repeats slogans." (Riding, 1983:32) García Márquez replies that the above-the-fray, critical position of Paz, Vargas Llosa, et al., "is the easy way out, because it is abstract. You just declare principles, and that's enough. You don't have to deal with reality that way, not even with the viability of your own principles." (Riding, 1983:40)

PLAGIARISM OF BALZAC?

Negative appraisals of his fiction are much more rare. At one point Miguel Angel Asturias, the Guatemalan writer (1899–

1974) and the only Latin American novelist to previously win the Nobel Prize, claimed that *One Hundred Years of Solitude* includes a plagiarism of Honore de Balzac's novels of 1830s Paris (see Janes, 1981 for mention of this **episode**). The general reaction to Asturias' charge was like Gerineldo Márquez's reaction to Colonel Aureliano Buendia, on the last occasion that the colonel proposes a revolution: "We knew you were old, Miguel Angel, but until now we hadn't realized just how old you were." (Asturias was miffed because García Márquez had poked fun at the older writer's style and criticized his acceptance, in 1966, of an ambassadorial post from the Guatemalan dictatorship.)

NOT REALISTIC ENOUGH?

The other criticism that has come up frequently (more from journalists than from literary critics) is the kind that Carballo's essay (1966) refuted, that García Márquez's style was not realistic enough to promote revolution. However, as we pointed out in chapter II, García Márquez has other ways of promoting his cause. The only obligation of a writer, he has said repeatedly, is to write good books.

He seems still to hold by what he told Armando Duran in an interview almost twenty years ago (Duran, 1968): The ideal novel, he said then, "is an absolutely free novel, that disturbs not only for its political and social content, but also for its power to penetrate reality; and better yet if it is able to flip over reality to turn it inside out, to show what it is like on the other side."

"Magic realism," then, is a way of making us really see reality by jarring us loose from our preconceptions.

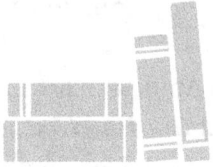

ONE HUNDRED YEARS OF SOLITUDE

ESSAY QUESTIONS AND ANSWERS

Question: *One Hundred Years of Solitude* has been called a "total novel" (Vargas Llosa) and a "perfect novel" (Carballo). What do these claims mean, and are they justified?

Answer: "Total" and "perfect" imply rather different things, the first having to do with the scope of the novel, the second with the fit of fictional ends and means. When Vargas Llosa called *One Hundred Years of Solitude* a "total novel," he went on to explain that it was "in the line of those insanely ambitious creations that aspire to compete with reality as an equal, facing it with an image of a qualitatively equal vitality, vastness and complexity"

First, the book has vitality because it is fast-moving - a "good read," as booksellers say. In fact, it moves a great deal faster than most people's real lives; the colonel's thirty-two rebellious wars occur so fast we don't even see them, but we see him at intervals and after they are all over. The transformation of Macondo by the banana company takes place in just a couple of paragraphs, although it must have been a process of several years. Finally, the destruction of Macondo and of the last of the Buendias, together with the deciphering of the mysterious manuscripts, sweeps by in about a page and a half.

Second, the novel is also vast in scope. On the most obvious level, the novel is "total," or complete, because it tells the entire story of the town of Macondo and of the Buendia Iguaran family from beginning to extermination. Of course, many novels are complete in this sense, but Vargas Llosa is getting at something more. He seems to be referring to the feeling readers get that they are reading about far more than one family's saga in a little town. Macondo seems to stand for all of Latin America or even as (Mario Benedetti suggested) the world. This is because its historical **themes** include the major transformation of the modern world, from mud huts to contemporary cities, and its psychological **themes** include the universal concerns about power and corruption, love and solitude, memory and myth, growth and decay (to name only a few). To readers from the many traditional environments similar to Macondo, whether in Latin America or other regions, the book will recall images that are then completed from the readers' own memories and imagination, making the experience seem still larger.

Vargas Llosa's third aspect of totality is "complexity." Not only are there scores of characters with many complicated schemes and ambitions, there is also an unusual degree of narrative complexity to the book. Several different kinds of language, or discourse, are heard or alluded to, from the sermons of a naive priest and the countersermons of the mad Jose Arcadio Buendia (delivered in Latin!), to government proclamations and war communiques by telegraph, to the shouts of strikers and the babel of newcomers to the Buendia house, and so on. Most complex of all is the use of the image of the manuscripts, first as a curiosity, then as an obsession of generations of Buendia men, then finally as the revelation, and reversal, of the text, so that at the end the book we have been reading becomes the book the characters have been trying to decode - or does it? This ambiguity, too, is like reality in its complexity of messages.

One Hundred Years of Solitude has also been called a "perfect" novel, meaning that its "structure, story, characters and style fully achieve their object" (Carballo, 1969:37). If García Márquez's object is to create the kind of complexity we have just discussed, then the repetitions of similar (but never identical) events, the continual looking forward and backward in time (through flashforwards and flashbacks), and the casting of doubt on the reliability of information are all highly appropriate devices in the structure and style of the novel. If the object is to create a **metaphor** for the history of Latin America, the story line - a little town and a family, from beginning to bitter end - is perfect. If the object is to make the readers have a good time, the characters with their extravagant obsessions and appetites for sex, food, and knowledge, are among the most successful ever invented.

Question: It has been suggested that García Márquez imagines a particular kind of reader of this book. What kind? And how does he (a) convey this idea and (b) induce the actual reader (you or me) to play the role of the ideal reader? Give specific examples.

Answer: In *One Hundred Years of Solitude*, García Márquez seems to want to make the reader his accomplice in understanding the story. The tone is one of taking the reader into the author's confidence, offering advance information on things that are about to happen and sharing gossip about the characters that they or the other characters are unaware of. The reader is supposed to become an active partner of the author's, figuring out more than he or she is being told.

García Márquez uses two main techniques for inducing the reader to become active in this way. First is the use of a naive narrative voice, recounting astonishing events. For example, the narrator tells us, quite calmly, that Father Nicanor Reyna levitates twelve centimeters after drinking hot chocolate, that Jose Arcadio (the firstborn son) is shot in the ear and that his blood winds its way through town to his mother's feet, that Remedios the beautiful grows suddenly pale and rises to heaven with the bedsheets, and, finally, that a child is born with a pig's tail. The reader knows that there must be more to these events than what the narrator tells us, some further meaning than the literal event itself. But, since the narrator is silent on what that meaning may be, he has activated the reader's imagination to find a satisfactory solution.

The second technique is the insertion of clues to an alternative reading of the book. As examples of one sort of clue, the characters themselves frequently comment on the repetitions of events, and the literal repetition of names strongly suggests a pattern to events. But this pattern must be inferred by the reader by piecing together the clues. It is not spelled out until near the end of the book, and then in terms that the reader may miss if he or she is not alert: the ancient Pilar Ternera perceives that the "axle" gets worn away as time "spins," meaning that while similar things occur over and over, the force holding them together deteriorates and the process must eventually come to an end.

Another set of very important clues has to do with reading a text. We are given hints to this **theme** from the strong emphasis on Melquiades and his manuscripts, from the third chapter onward. Jose Arcadio Buendia's attempt to build a memory machine seems also to have something to do with reading. Colonel Aureliano Buendia writes poetry but then, in his bitter retirement, burns it all, perhaps because it reveals something that would threaten his solitude; the texts of the government perform the magic feat of making the workers nonexistent, and after the strikers are killed, of eliminating that event from history. There is also an English encyclopedia that gives access to knowledge. All these clues suggest that the reader must not take what he or she is reading at face value, because written texts are mysterious, ambiguous and unreliable. In case there was any doubt, the Catalan book dealer declares in the last chapter that "literature is the best toy ever invented to fool people." By now, we the readers should really be on our toes.

If we have been alert to these clues, then we will be prepared to put things together when it is discovered that everything we have been reading is included in the manuscripts of Melquiades that generations of Buendias have been trying to read. Some of us may have caught on long before, most of us will be surprised at the final revelation but, thinking back on all the clues, will see that it makes sense. Not the kind of sense of the real world, of course - books don't literally self-destruct when we understand them - but fictional sense, because it fits in with the imaginary world that García Márquez has created and, now, destroyed.

Question: "Magic **realism**" is a term often applied to García Márquez's fiction. What does the term mean, and how does it apply to *One Hundred Years of Solitude*? What is its purpose? Illustrate your argument with examples.

Answer: "Magic **realism**" refers to the description of improbable or impossible events (magic) in the clear, calm, sharply focused language expected in realistic reporting. The description will often include very precise physical details that give an illusion of realism.

There are many examples of impossible or improbable events in *One Hundred Years of Solitude*, almost all of them treated in this realistic way.

First, it will be helpful to look at the one major exception, a magical event that is treated unrealistically, to illustrate (by contrast) the technique. This is the final destruction of Macondo, the manuscripts, and the Buendia family, where the language as well as the events are magical. Aureliano, who has not moved from the spot where he has first seen his dead son, suddenly "sees" the epigraph of the manuscripts - there is no mention of his going to fetch them, or of what the binding or the handwriting looks like; actually, there is no suggestion at all that what he "sees" is really, materially, before him.

Then, after "seeing" their epigraph, he does get the manuscripts, and we are told what they are like physically:

> **He found them intact, among the prehistoric plants and steaming puddles and luminous insects which had banished from the room all vestige of the passage of men on the earth, and he did not have the serenity to take them out to the light, but right there, standing, without the least difficulty, as though they had been written in Spanish under the brilliant light of midday, he began to decipher them aloud.**

There are some realistic details, but overall, the narration is wondrous, breathless, as Aureliano speed-reads through the manuscripts and finally comes to the conclusion which is pure magic, in fact, a magic formula:

> **Nevertheless, before he reached the final verse he had already understood that he would never leave**

that room, for it was foreseen that the city of mirrors (or of mirages) would be wiped away by the wind and banished from the memory of men in the instant that Aureliano Babilonia finished deciphering the manuscripts, and that everything written in them was unrepeatable from always and for always, because the bloodlines condemned to one hundred years of solitude do not have a second opportunity on earth. (490–492)

Why? What is the connection between deciphering and disappearing? We simply have to trust that it is so, as in a fairy tale.

In contrast, the levitation of Father Nicanor Reyna is treated as something not particularly wonderful at all. First, the priest's powers are severely limited: he can rise only twelve centimeters. (The precision of the figure is one of García Márquez's tricks to give a semblance of **realism** to the anecdote.) Second, he can rise only if he first drinks hot chocolate (more "realistic" detail). Finally, the mad Jose Arcadio Buendia scoffs at this supposed miracle and tells him, in Latin, that there is nothing to it - which seems to deflate the priest. The purpose of the anecdote seems more to demonstrate the credulity of the townspeople, who are willing to believe this miracle, than to demonstrate Nicanor's powers.

Similarly, when Remedios the beautiful ascends to heaven, she does not simply mysteriously rise. The ascension takes place at a precise time, an afternoon when she and Fernanda go out to hang up sheets. She does not rise without warning: first she becomes very pale, almost transparent, and reports that she feels fine. And she does not rise alone: the sheets flutter up to heaven with her. All of this is impossible in the real world, but the physical details and the comedy - the rising of the sheets and the dismay of Fernanda - give the anecdote a tone of realistic reporting.

The purpose of this anecdote seems to be twofold: to further delineate the character of Fernanda (who is both jealous of Remedios and angry that God stole her sheets), and to carry the **metaphor** of Remedios's purity to its logical conclusion, that is, within the fantastic logic of the novel, where everything is taken to extremes.

There is another rhetorical device in the novel, which is almost the reverse of the kind of "magic **realism**" in the stories of Nicanor and Remedios: the magical treatment of a realistic event. For example, at the very beginning of the book there is an account of an event which is not impossible or improbable at all, but in fact was repeated many thousands of times throughout the Americas: the establishment of a pioneer village on the bank of a river. But this realistic event is recounted in the language of magic: the stones of the river are "polished, white and enormous, like prehistoric eggs," and the "world was so new, many things did not have names..." Here the language seeks to recapture the impression the pioneers themselves had of their environment. Later on, in the **episode** of the massacre of the strikers, magic and realism are thoroughly mixed together: the actual, historical words of the commanding general are used, along with a fantastic account of the number of casualties (three thousand, more than the whole town could have had) and of the train carrying the bodies to the sea.

By using these techniques of "magic realism," García Márquez is able to heighten the effects of his episodes, making them either funnier or more tragic. More important, they prevent us from taking the story at its most mundane, literal level. The "magic **realism**" tells us that the tale stands for something else, something bigger. In part, like a fairy tale, it is a fable about human nature. And more than that, like a great historical **epic** full of realistic detail, it is a reminder of some very large historical events in Latin America and the world.

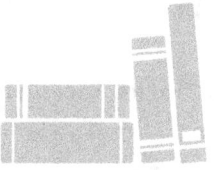

BIBLIOGRAPHY

WORKS BY GABRIEL GARCÍA MÁRQUEZ

One Hundred Years Of Solitude

1967 *Cien anos de soledad*. 1st ed., Buenos Aires: Editorial Sudamericana, 1967. The first edition, from which all later editions of this publisher were made. Also published by *Edhasa*, in Barcelona (1968), "por cuenta y orden de Editorial Sudamericana." There have been at least five other editions in Spanish (Barcelona, Madrid [two], Havana [two], at least one of which has gone through six printings), and translations in twenty-five languages, including Croatian and Farsi.

1984 *Cien anos de soledad, edicion de Jacques Joset*. Madrid: Ediciones Catedra, Letras Hispanicas. The edition used in this Monarch Note study guide.

Other Fiction

1955 *La hojarasca*. Bogota: Ediciones Sipa.

1961 *El coronel no tiene quien le escriba*. Medellin, Colombia: Aguirre Editor.

1962 *Los funerales de la Mama Grande*. Xalapa, Mexico: Editorial Universidad Veracruzana. Includes: "La siesta del martes," "Un dia de estos," "En este pueblo no hay ladrones," "La prodigiosa tarde de Baltazar," "La viuda de Montiel," "Un dia despues del sabado," "Rosas artificiales," "Los funerales de la Mama Grande."

1962 *La mala hora*. Madrid: Talleres de Graficas Luis Perez.

1967 *Isabel viendo llover en Macondo*. Buenos Aires: Editorial Estuario.

1972 *La increible y triste historia de la candida Erendira y de su abuela desalmada*. Barcelona: Barral Editores. Includes: "Un senor muy viejo con unas alas enormes," "El mar del tiempo perdido," "El ahogado mas hermoso del mundo," "Muerte constante mas alla del amor," "El ultimo viaje del buque fantasma," "Blacaman el bueno vendedor de milagros," "La increible y triste historia de la candida Erendira y de su abuela desalmada."

1972 *El negro que hizo esperar a los angeles*. Montevideo: Ediciones Alfil. Includes: "Nabo, el negro que hizo esperar a los angeles," "Alguien desordena estas rosas," "La mujer que llegaba a las seis," "Ojos de perro azul," "Dialogo del espejo," "Amargura para tres sonambulos," "Eva esta dentro de su gato," "La otra costilla de la muerte," "La tercera resignacion."

1972 *Ojos de perro azul*. Rosario, Argentina: Equiseditorial. Same stories as above, but in reverse order, plus: "La noche de los alcaravanes," "Monologo de Isabel viendo llover en Macondo." Cuatro cuentos. Mexico: *Comunidad Latinoamerica de Escritores*.

1975 *El otono del patriarca*. Barcelona: Plaza y Janes.

1975 *Todos los cuentos de Gabriel García Márquez* (1947–1972). Barcelona: Plaza y Janes.

1980? *Cronica de una muerte anunciada*. La Habana: Casa de las Americas.

1985 *El amor en los tiempos del colera*. Mexico: Editorial Diana.

Fiction In English Translation

1968 *No One Writes to the Colonel and Other Stories*. Trans. J.S. Bernstein. New York: Harper & Row.

1970 *One Hundred Years of Solitude*. Trans. Gregory Rabassa. New York: Harper & Row.

1972 *Leafstorm and Other Stories*. Trans. Gregory Rabassa. New York: Harper & Row.

1976 *The Autumn of the Patriarch*. Trans. Gregory Rabassa. New York: Harper & Row.

1979 *In Evil Hour*. New York: Avon Bard.

1979 *Innocent Erendira and Other Stories*. New York: Harper Colophon Books.

1982 *Chronicle of a Death Foretold*. New York: Alfred A. Knopf.

Nonfiction (Essays And Articles)

1957 *De viaje por los paises socialistas*. 90 dias en la "Cortina de Hierro." Bogota: Editorial La Oveja Negra, 6a. edicion, 1981. Eleven articles reprinted from the magazines *Cromos* (Colombia) and *Momento* (Venezuela), where they first appeared in 1957. They report on Gabriel García Márquez's encounters and observations during trips to East Germany, Czechoslovakia, Poland, Hungary, and USSR. See Chapter II of this Note for discussion.

1968 *La novela en America Latina: Dialogo, con Mario Vargas Llosa.* Lima: Carlos Milla Batres.

1970 *Relato de un naufrago.* Barcelona: Tusquets Editor.

1973 *Cuando era feliz e indocumentado.* Caracas: Ediciones El Ojo del Camello.

1976 *Cronicas y reportajes.* Bogota: Insituto Colombiano de Cultura.

1977 *Operacion Carlota.* Lima: Mosca Azuel.

1978 *Periodismo militante.* Bogota: Son de maquina Editores.

1980 "Breves nostalgias sobre Juan Rulfo." Pages 23–26 in *Inframundo: el Mexico de Juan Rulfo* (eds. anonymous). *Ediciones del Norte*, 1983; first edition, Instituto de Bellas Artes (Mexico), 1980. Gabriel García Márquez recalls his first stay in Mexico (1961?), where he supported his family (poorly) by a radio program on, or as the Colombian ambassador complained, "against" Colombian literature and where he first encountered the works of Rulfo (learning Pedro Paramo by memory) and worked on filmscripts of Rulfo's El gallo de oro and Pedro Paramo. Difficulties of translating the latter to film made Gabriel García Márquez conscious of Rulfo's manipulations of chronological ambiguities, as well as the importance of names (especially in fiction) in defining character (film actors are hardly ever adequate to the images suggested by the names).

1982 *Obra periodistica.* 3 vols. Barcelona: Bruguera. Newspaper columns and articles from the early days.

1986 *La aventura de Miguel Littin clandestino en Chile.* Mexico: Editorial Diana.

INTERVIEWS AND JOURNALISTIC REPORTS

García Márquez, Gabriel

1981 "The Art of Fiction: Interview with Gabriel García Márquez." *The Paris Review*, LXXXII, 69. García Márquez remarks that the Faulknerian influence has been exaggerated, that it was really "a coincidence: I had simply found material that had to be dealt with in the same way that Faulkner had treated similar material." 52–53 (Cited in Levitt, in Shaw 1986)

Dreifus, Claudia

1983 "Playboy Interview: Gabriel García Márquez." *Playboy*, February: 65ff. Interview took place in May, 1981, in Paris, where "for nine days, we talked, argued and parried." (66)

Duran, Armando

1968 "Entrevista a García Márquez." *Revista Nacional de Cultura de Caracas*, Nr. 185.

Fernandez-Braso, Miguel

1982 *La soledad de Gabriel García Márquez. Una conversacion infinita.* Barcelona: Editorial Planeta. 150 p. First edition, Madrid: Editorial Azur, 1969 (January). First Spanish reporter to interview García Márquez in Barcelona, 1968.

García M., Eligio

1982 "GGM: El poder y la gloria." Pages 89–122 in *Son asi: Reportaje a nueve escritores latinoamericanos*. Bogota: Editorial La Oveja Negra. Three reports on García Márquez by his younger brother, a newspaper reporter. I. "El circulo de tiza" (1st pub. in Bogota magazine *Flash*, Feb. 1971, unsigned): interview of GGM at their parents' home in Cartagena; Eligio concludes that his brother, frightened and irritated by his sudden fame, has drawn a chalk circle around himself like Colonel Aureliano Buendia at the height of his power; tone of article suggests that Eligio felt himself outside that circle; II. "Bienvenidos, senoras y senores, al reino de Macondo" (1972): funny, irreverent account of seven-day "fiesta de la cultura" in Caracas to bestow the Romulo Gallegos prize (Bs. 100.000) on author of the best Latin American novel of the previous five years. Everybody knows (even the innocent Erendira, according to a Caracas cartoonist) that the prize will go to Gabriel García Márquez for *Cien anos de soledad*. GGM creates a scandal of sorts when he turns the prize money over to the Movimiento al Socialismo (MAS), an independent leftist party. III. "La primavera feliz en Paris del patriarca García Márquez" (1975): While Gabriel García Márquez is busy at his political writings, saying he won't produce any more novels for a while ("se acabo la gasolina por lo pronto" [I've run out of gasoline for now], he says), Eligio reflects on the hard work of Carmen Balcells, GGM's agent, who sold *Cien anos de soledad* after publishers in Spain and Mexico had turned it down.

Mendoza, Plinio Apuleyo

1982 *El olor de la guayaba. Conversaciones con Plinio Apuleyo Mendoza*. Bogota: Editorial la Oveja Negra. 133 pages. Very important for background to *One Hundred Years of Solitude*.

Riding, Alan

1983 "Revolution and the Intellectual in Latin America." *New York Times Magazine*, v. 132, May 13, p. 28(10). Discusses García Márquez' politics and those of his intellectual opponents, especially Octavio Paz.

LITERARY CRITICISM OF ONE HUNDRED YEARS OF SOLITUDE (SELECTED)

Abenoza, Bianca Ossorio de

1979 *Gabriel García Márquez juzgado por la critica: una bibliografia analitica y comentada*, 1955-1974. University of Virginia Ph.D. dissertation. 373 pages. The section on *One Hundred Years of Solitude*, p. 259-316.

Benedetti, Mario, et al. (Contributors)

1969 *[Nueve] asedios a García Márquez*. Santiago de Chile: Editorial Universitaria, s.a. Bib. Essays by Mario Benedetti, Emmanuel Carballo, Pedro Lastra, Juan Loveluck, Julio Ortega, Jose Miguel Oviedo, Angel Rama, Mario Vargas Llosa, and Ernesto Volkening; all but Oviedo's and Vargas Llosa's reprinted from earlier publications. Handy collection of some of the earliest reactions in Latin America to Cien anos de soledad. The bibliography (pages 174-182) is annotated and in two sections, "Obras" (Works) of García Márquez and "Referencias" (reviews and studies), with summaries.

Benedetti, Mario

1967 "Gabriel García Márquez o la vigilia dentro del sueno." In Benedetti et al., 1969, pp. 11-21. Reprinted from *Letras del continente mestizo*. Montevideo: Arca, 1967, pp. 145-154.

Caballo, Emmanuel

1967 "Gabriel García Márquez, un gran novelista Latinoamericano." In Benedetti et al., 1969:22-37. Reprinted from *Revista de la Universidad de Mexico* 12, 3 (noviembre 1967): 10-16.

Farias, Victor

1981 *Los manuscritos de Melquiades: "Cien Anos de Soledad", burguesia latinoamericana y dialectica de la reproduccion.* Frankfurt/Main: Verlag Klaus Dieter Vervuert. 404 pages. Chapter-by-chapter analysis along lines suggested by subtitle ("Latin American bourgoisie, and dialectics of reproduction"), with stress on Hegel's concept of negation - specifically, that solitude is the negation of solidarity.

Incledon, John

1986 "Writing and Incest in *One Hundred Years of Solitude.*" In Shaw and Vera-Godwin, 1986:51-64.

Janes, Regina

1981 *Gabriel García Márquez: Revolutions in Wonderland.* Columbia, MO: University of Missouri Press. 115 pages. Excellent analysis of GGM's struggle with literary technique up to and beyond the writing of *One Hundred Years of Solitude.* See discussion in Chapter VI of this Note.

Joset, Jacques

1984 "Introduccion" to annotated edition of *Cien anos de soledad*, pp. 9–44. Madrid: Ediciones Catedra.

Lastra, Pedro

1966 "La tragedia como fundamento estructural de La hojarasca." Benedetti et al, 1969:38–51, from *Anales de la Universidad de Chile* 124, 140 (oct-dic 1966):168–186. *Analysis of a novel*, Lu hojarasca, that may be considered as an experimental study for *One Hundred Years of Solitude*.

Levitt, Morton P.

1986 "From **Realism** to Magic Realism: The Meticulous Modernist Fictions of García Márquez." Shaw and Vera-Godwin, 1986:73–89.

Loveluck, Juan

1966 "Gabriel García Márquez, narrador colombiano." Benedetti et al., 1969:52–73, from *Duquesne Hispanic Review* 5, 3 (1966):135–154. (On La hojarasca.)

Ludmer, Josefina

1972 *Cien anos de soledad: una interpretacion*. Buenos Aires: Tiempo Contemporaneo.

McMurray, George

1977 *Gabriel García Márquez*. New York: Frederick Ungar.

Minta, Stephen

1987 *Gabriel García Márquez: Writer of Colombia*. New York: Harper and Row. 197 pages. Describes the Colombian historical and social context of GGM's work. Interesting detail on the War of a Thousand Days and General Rafael Uribe Uribe, the prototype of Col. Aureliano Buendia. Chapters V and VI (pp. 144–179), on *One Hundred Years of Solitude*, are interesting mainly for their comparison of GGM's fictional accounts with the history of the real events, especially the wars and the banana strike. The literary observations are not acute.

Oberhelman, Harley D.

1980 *The Presence of Faulkner in the Writings of García Márquez*. Lubbock TX: Texas Tech Press. 43 pages. Establishes that García Márquez's first reading of Faulkner occurred about 1947 and that he read and discussed Faulkner's writings carefully. Good summary of about all that needs to be said on the topic. See García Márquez's remarks in *The Paris Review*, 1981.

Ortega, Julio

1968 "Gabriel García Márquez/Cien anos de soledad." Benedetti et al., 1969:74–88, from *La contemplacion y la fiesta* (ensayos). Lima: Editorial Universitaria, 1968:44–58.

Palencia-Roth, Michael

1986 "Prisms of Consciousness: The 'New Worlds' of Columbus and García Márquez." Shaw and Vera Godwin, 1986:15–32.

Pinard, Mary C.

1986 "Time in and out of Solitude in *One Hundred Years of Solitude*." Shaw and Vera-Godwin, 1986:65–72

Rama, Angel

1969 "Un novelista de la violencia americana." Benedetti et al., 1969:106–125. "La primera parte... levemente corregida" from article in *Marcha 1*, 201 (April 17, 1964):22–23.

Rama, Angel, and Mario Vargas Llosa

1973 *García Márquez y la problematica de la novela*. Buenos Aires: Ediciones Corregidor. 89 pages.

Shaw, Bradley A. and Nora Vera-Godwin, eds.

1986 *Critical Perspectives on Gabriel García Márquez*. Lincoln, Nebraska: Society of Spanish and Spanish American Studies. 159 pages. Bibliography, Preface, and nine essays.

Sims, Robert L.

1986 "Matriarchal and Patriarchal Patterns in GGM's Leaf Storm, 'Big Mama's Funeral' and *One Hundred Years of Solitude*: The Synergetic, Mythic and Bricolage Synthesis." Shaw and Vera Godwin, 1986:33–50.

Vadillo, Alfonso

1984 *La astilla del tiempo*. Mexico: Martin Casillas Editores. 111 pages. Uses Cien anos de soledad as a model of a Gramscian conception of social development.

Vargas Llosa, Mario

1969 "García Márquez: de Aracataca a Macondo." In Benedetti et al., 1969, pp. 126–146.

1971 *Gabriel García Márquez: historia de un deicidio*. Barcelona: Barral; Caracas: Monte Avila. (See discussion in chapter VI of this study.)

Verges, Salvador

1973 *El problema de Dios en Cien anos de soledad*. Bogota: Ediciones Paulina.

Volkening, Ernesto

1963 "Gabriel García Márquez o el tropico desembrujado." Benedetti et al., 1969:147–173, from *Revista de la Cultura de Occidente* (Bogota), 7, 4 (agosto 1963):275–293. Macondo as a South American Yoknapatawpha County (William Faulkner's invented region in Mississippi).

(Vosgos Publishers - Anonymous Author)

1978 *Cien anos de soledad. Gabriel García Márquez. Compendios Vosgos No 37.* Barcelona: Editorial Vosgos. 101 pages. Chapter-by-chapter synopsis and commentary, very detailed. Also includes an alphabetical listing, with brief description, of every character in the novel and of many of the unusual terms.

Williams, Raymond L.

1984 *Gabriel García Márquez.* Boston: Twayne Publishers. 157 pages. Notes, bibliography.

LITERARY THEORY

Bakhtin, Mikhail

1981 *The Dialogic Imagination.* Austin: University of Texas Press. Insightful and immensely broad study of novelistic technique from ancient to contemporary times, in every culture that produced something that could be called a "novel." Particularly relevant to *One Hundred Years of Solitude* is Bakhtin's concept of heteroglossia: language as continuous flux of incorporated languages, as opposed to concept of static unitary language. Dialogism: mode of a world dominated by heteroglossia. Cf. Williams, 1984, for discussion of this concept in relation to García Márquez.

Steiner, George

1978 *On Difficulty and Other Essays.* Oxford University Press. The title essay will be especially valuable for understanding the various kinds of "difficulty" the student may be having in reading *One Hundred Years of Solitude.*

EXPLORE THE ENTIRE LIBRARY OF BRIGHT NOTES STUDY GUIDES

From Shakespeare to Sinclair Lewis and from Plato to Pearl S. Buck, The Bright Notes Study Guide library spans hundreds of volumes, providing clear and comprehensive insights into the world's greatest literature. Discover more, faster with the Bright Notes Study Guide to the classics you're reading today.

See the entire library of available
Bright Notes guides at **BrightNotes.com**

Available in print and digital wherever books are sold

IP INFLUENCE PUBLISHERS

www.ingramcontent.com/pod-product-compliance
Lightning Source LLC
LaVergne TN
LVHW011709060526
838200LV00051B/2826